PAID ON FRIDAY, BROKE

BY TUESDAY

The Pathway To Unstoppable Success

Felecia Higgs Walker

ISBN 9798856879635

Printed by Epiphany Publishing

11180 Highway 51 S STE. 7

Atoka, TN 38004

Dedication

To Dante, Zyon, and Auston:

You will FOREVER be my reasons WHY!

Thank you for riding with me!

Mama Loves You!

About me

Hi, I'm Felecia! Founder and CEO of The Focus Group by Felecia LLC. Executive Career Coach/ Business Coach/ Career Course Creator/ Motivational Speaker/ Podcast Host and now Author.

I earned both my Bachelors and Masters degrees in Social Work from the University of Tennessee, Knoxville. As a single mother of three sons, I believe in the value of continued education, but I also stand behind the non-traditional career path population.

My career progression business focuses on the professional, life changing work it takes to land the job of your dreams and elevate your career to the highest level. I help people learn how to identify their WHY, learn the Art of Networking, and how to Master the Job Interview. I am committed to helping others change their lives through real world career guidance.

Throughout this book, you will develop the tools and confidence you need to succeed. My goal is to empower you to become the person you want to be. You are unique and your coaching should be too. We will start where you are and work towards your goals.

Felecia Higgs Walker

Table of Contents

We Just Wanted Tacos...

Have you ever had the smallest moment that was the straw that broke the camel's back?

I have.

Allow me to share with you the broken moment that broke me down and woke me up at the same time.

This moment changed my life forever. This moment changed my core and gave me the motivation to be different and to separate myself from the pack.

I call it my Kroger moment.

I can clearly remember it; it was a Tuesday. With $25 in the bank, $3 in my purse and payday happening at the end of the week, my children and I stopped at the grocery store with our stomachs ready for tacos. My sons grabbed all the fixings of a great meal and I, on the other hand, was subtracting the cost of every item.

Have you ever had that moment in the store when you are using all of your math skills to calculate each item because you know you have a limited budget?

We got to the register and my bill was $21.17.

I had calculated correctly. We could have tacos. It was going to be a good night.

But all of a sudden, I heard the beep when I checked out. My card had declined. I stared at the screen and asked the clerk to scan it again.

My card was declined twice.

I frantically checked my bank balance and saw that a popular streaming service had kindly withdrawn their monthly service fee.

There was now $5 in my account, and I was forced to leave the entire basket of groceries in the store.

Can you imagine how I felt, especially being in front of my children? I was embarrassed, ashamed, and I felt like a failure. My son asked, "What happened to the food?" I explained that I didn't have enough money, but we could stop at a fast food restaurant to order burgers from the dollar menu.

They didn't notice, but I didn't eat that night.

How many times have you sacrificed yourself for someone else?

As a parent, it is our responsibility, but when do we take responsibility for what is happening in our life?

That moment broke me, but it also woke me at the same time. I tattooed that moment on my brain.

Yes. That moment pushed me past personal and professional obstacles that could have glued my feet to the ground.

I was changed forever.

Oddly enough, the entire day before I picked my boys up from school, I spent the morning volunteering at Toys for Tots, packing Christmas toys for children in need.

Little did I know that just hours later I would be face down and crying in my office, asking God to help me, asking God to change my circumstances and the job I was working.

I needed my life to change, and I was ready to do the work.

I know we are just getting started, but do me a favor, take a moment and write down a couple of your broken moments that have changed your life. Then write down a short list of people who are dependent on you. Lastly, write down a few goals that will change your life and theirs.

Oftentimes, the steps needed to elevate your life don't become real to us until we write them down.

Your Broken Moments:

_____

_____

_____

_____

_____

Your People:

_____

_____

_____

_____

_____

Your Goals:

_____

_____

_____

_____

_____

To be honest with you, my WHY is so big: it consists of my children, my mother, my uncle, my family. I can go on and on about how much I love them and how I want to create some amazing experiences for them, but instead I'll just show you.

Now, I would like for you to write down how you felt during those broken moments.

Give your moment a name. Once you name your moment, write down how you felt as if you were telling the story to someone who needed to be encouraged.

It's okay if you start to relive the emotion you felt. It's okay if tears start to fall, let them fall and don't wipe them away. Sit in the moment, understand what pain you felt during that moment.

This is the moment that is going to change your life. It is this moment that will become the foundation in which you make all of your future decisions. It will become that thing that you never want to experience ever again. This moment in your life will be what pushes you to greatness.

Hello and Welcome!

Welcome to the Focus Group by Felecia, a real-world career coaching company for job seekers, entry to mid level employees, and high school and college students.

So sometimes in life, our world gets turned upside down and it feels like we can't catch our breath. It feels like the people we depend on turn away from us, and we feel alone.

Sometimes, everything we try fails and we lose our confidence. Sometimes, life requires us to hit the reset button in order to get our lives, our careers, and our families back on track. Well, regardless of what knocks you down, I'm saying to you now and for the rest of the book, get up and try again!

Because you are reading this book, I can only guess that you need something to change in your life and I can assure you that I am here to help.

My mission is to live out God's purpose for my life, by helping others to become the best version of themselves. I've been knocked down a few times in my life, but each time I fought like hell to get back up. Bringing a focus to my focus, change my life. And I promise if you commit to doing the work, this book will do the same for you! Are you ready? Then let's go!

Now, I want to go a little deeper into who I am and why I am so confident that my blueprint can and will change your life. There's a quote by Les Brown, which has become a guiding principle for how I live my life and it says...

QUOTE:

You must be willing to do the things today others won't do in order to have the things tomorrow others won't have. - Les Brown

Exactly what the quote says, is exactly what I had to do. I had to walk and talk differently. I had to volunteer for projects and committees that I really didn't want to be a part of. Was it worth it? Absolutely! Will it be worth it for you? Absolutely!

Over the past 25 years, I have developed a passion for encouraging and empowering others do not give up on themselves and to live up to their maximum potential. Another quote by Les Brown, which has become a guiding principle for how I live my life says,

Quote: To have what you've never had and do things that you've never done; You must become someone you've never been! – Les Brown

My Story

If you have never had to wait by the phone for the dreaded call from your employer, only to find out the fate of your family's livelihood, be thankful. Take it from someone who has been through two corporate layoffs, these moments can be paralyzing and filled with so much uncertainty.

For me, the call came on March 30th, 2017, at that time, I was a pharmaceutical sales representative with 10 years of experience. Although 10 years seems like a long time to be with a company, I still was fairly new to the pharmaceutical industry. The phrases: branded drugs, generic, and patent expirations, were all a part of my daily conversations and sales language. However, I really didn't know how those words would impact the future of my sales job.

The clock struck 9:00 AM and my manager's name appeared on my phone. "I'm sorry Felecia, but you are on the list to be let go." To be honest, I was very aware of the layoff possibility, but hearing the actual words still stung and caused a bit of anxiety. This was the moment that would change my life and send me on a professional roller coaster.

I would go on to take a 60% pay cut with my next job, but then through intentional career progression, I would triple my salary over the next three years. As I earned my first promotion and later returned to the pharmaceutical industry, I felt in my gut that I wasn't there to stay. I truly believe that God had blessed me to go through all the professional lessons, successes, and failures so that I could teach others how to progress their own careers and change their lives.

I wish someone would have provided me with an interview, networking, and professional development blueprint. Instead, God blessed me with the foresight to build my own blueprint for success and now I have the courage and the platform to share it with you.

I hope my book and my story will not only motivate you to progress in your career, but provide the necessary steps to change your life, no matter your situation.

I wish I could tell you that my story began in 2017 when I was laid off from my 6 figure salaried pharmaceutical sales job, but that would be a complete lie. If I can be honest, the foundation of my story began before my feet touched down on the college campus of the University of Tennessee, Knoxville in 1991. When I was in high school my mother kept saying "when you go to college, when you go to college." So, I knew I was going to college, but had no idea of why I was going or what to do when I got there.

I initially majored in accounting because two of my uncles were accountants, but that was not my calling. LOL! My grandmother was a nurse, but all of my life I watched her work the third shift at the hospital and sleep the next day away. Her job definitely took care of the bills but from my perspective, it didn't allow her to enjoy her life. As a result, to an 18 year old young woman, that was not the life I desired.

I've always known, ever since I was a child, that I loved helping others and that's what stuck as my major. I chose Human Services for undergraduate studies and social work for my master's degree. As it turns out, helping others was my calling, but I was clueless to all of the directions it would take me.

The majority of my colleagues were engineering majors, but because I didn't see, here, or know anything about that industry, I just assumed it wasn't for me. The type of salaries they earn right after graduation blew my mind and always kept me wondering "what if". After a while, I would just accept the fact that those type of jobs and salaries weren't meant for me. It wasn't until 2007, when the opportunity to transfer my social work skill set to pharmaceutical sales, when the belief even entered my mind that I could do something different and live a different life. This was the first time I believed that $50,000 wasn't the most amount of money I could make on a job. This was the beginning of the mindset that I could, I deserved, and I was worthy of having more.

Over the next 10 years my confidence would grow, my business acumen would be strengthened, and I would learn to enjoy life to the fullest. However, as life would have it sometimes, my world got flipped upside down and I was laid off from my job in 2017.

Although I put on a brave face and a fake smile, I was devastated and afraid of who I would be without that job. I lost $115,000 salary. I lost a company car. I lost my 401K plan. And I lost my flexibility. This next sentence is one that is not talked about a lot, but I believe it to be sadly true; without that salary, I lost my independence and my ability to have choices. I started to feel like a failure because my income level dropped.

I allowed those feelings of shame to keep me from getting back into the industry. Instead, I lied to myself by saying; "I don't need that job, I can't just go work somewhere else, and I can still take care of my children while taking a pay cut." Let me tell you, I was WRONG, WRONG, WRONG! Did I say WRONG? LOL!

The next four years would take me on an emotional roller coaster and send me on an uphill battle with my career. However, the sequence of amazing events that occurred on my way up is why I am confident I can help you today. I did things that I never thought I would do. I spoke to people I never thought I was worthy of speaking too. I disciplined myself in ways that I never thought possible, and I created a blueprint for a successful rise to greatness. My journey to success has not been easy, but I am grateful that I get to share it with you today. None of what you will read is for bragging purposes, but to inspire you to do what is necessary to change your life. So fasten your seat belt and let's begin this beautiful journey together. I believe in you!

Disclosure Statement

I am adding this disclosure statement because I don't want you to get to the end of the book and feel like you didn't get anything out of it. Trust me, I am giving you everything from A-Z, but it is up to you to do the work. This book was written to help you reach your next level. However, what I share with you will not work if you don't do the work. By the end of this book you will feel like we are best friends. You will have powerful breakthroughs and eye-opening moments, but if you don't leap into action, you will not see a change in your career or your life. You may be motivated by my advice, but if you don't take it and apply it to your own life, your life will not change. So be honest with yourself throughout the book, be committed to the work, and do what it takes to elevate your life.

My tone may sound pushy at times, but it's only because I know that you want something different in your life. No, I take that back. I know the reason you invested in this book is because you NEED something different in your life. I know what it's like to go to a job every day that you are not crazy about. On top of that you're not making the type of money you imagine yourself making. I know what that's like.

Take your time. Complete each Chapter. Don't rush, take as many notes as possible, and complete all activities. Cry if you need to, laugh if you want to, but believe in yourself and go land the job of your dreams. I am giving you everything and I want you to take it and turn your life into what you want it to be. Take this book, apply the knowledge, and turn your life into everything you desire. Let's go!

POWER WORD

Every chapter will have a power word that blazes the pathway to unstoppable success. I want you to meditate on these words as they are a roadmap to the next level in your life. The Power Word for this chapter is Conquest.

Conquest—this powerful word encapsulates the very essence of the journey I am about to share with you. Let me take you back to that life-changing moment, my "Kroger Moment," where a simple grocery run became a turning point that awakened a burning desire within me—to conquer life's challenges and soar to new heights of success.

In that unassuming store aisle, with my children by my side, all I wanted was to prepare a simple taco dinner. Little did I know that this moment would push me to the brink, financially and emotionally. With just $25 in the bank, $3 in my purse, and payday on the way, my heart raced as I tallied every item's cost.

But life had a different plan for me. My card declined— not once, but twice. A streaming service fee had swooped in, leaving me with a mere $5 in my account. I had no choice but to abandon the groceries we had so eagerly chosen.

In that moment, I felt the weight of shame, embarrassment, and failure press down upon me. But instead of succumbing to defeat, I found a new purpose— to conquer life's adversities and take charge of my own destiny.

"Conquest" became my guiding word, propelling me forward with unwavering determination. It symbolizes the courage to face challenges head-on, to rise above setbacks, and to mold my own future.

As I share my story with you, I invite you to embrace the spirit of "conquest." Let it ignite the fire within you—to break free from limitations, transcend self-doubt, and chart a course towards your own greatness.

This chapter's power word, "conquest," serves as a reminder that we have the power to transform our lives. It calls upon us to confront our broken moments, embrace our unique potential, and carve a path of triumph and empowerment.

Through "conquest," I hope to inspire you to reclaim control of your life, seize your dreams, and rewrite your destiny. Together, let's awaken the conqueror within and surge forward with unyielding determination.

As you continue reading, keep "conquest" at the forefront of your mind. It will guide you through the challenges that lie ahead, urging you to push beyond your limits and soar to new heights of success.

Prepare to embark on a journey of transformation, where "conquest" becomes your battle cry. Together, we will conquer the obstacles that come our way, and emerge as unstoppable forces of change.

Chapter 1

Your Why for Everything

Your Why for Everything

Understanding the core of who you are and why you operate the way you do is really the foundation of this book. It is important to understand your need to do better and be better. People always ask me, how in the world do you stay so motivated all the time? I tell them, it's because I know what and who I'm working for. See, once you understand your core beliefs and the why for everything you do it will not matter what you have to do in order to make those changes in your life. You will just move with no hesitation.

I believe that the core of who you are and your why for everything are built on broken moments in your life. Now, I'm not talking about those moments that pissed you off, but those moments that freaking rocked your world and brought you to your knees, and made you ask yourself how I got here?" I'm referring to those moments that you never saw coming and left you confused.

I'm referring to those moments where you have felt stuck in a job that stressed you out, didn't pay you enough money to pay your bills, and kept you away from your family. I'm talking about those moments where you cried yourself to sleep because you couldn't figure that thing out and you were afraid to share your struggles with those closest to you.

Those are the moments that make you take a long look in the mirror and say how can I change my life, what can I do differently, and enough is enough. I believe that these moments should be married to your goals, and I call this concept the Heart-Goal Connection.

The Heart-Goal Connection gives you permission to remember how you felt during those dark times and use that feeling as a motivator for change. Now, we don't want to dwell on those moments and remain in that self-pity state of mind, but we do want to remember that place and time you never want to visit again. Allow your heart to guide you to your goals.

This small segment of the book will help you do some real soul searching and reveal what needs to change in your life. This section should provide you with a few tips on how to change your life and prepare yourself for what's to come.

So now that you understand how those broken moments made you feel, let's concentrate on those people who are depending on you to change your life. Because if you change your life you changed their lives. I'm talking about your spouse, your children, your parents, your family, or your community. That's your core. That's who is dependent on you to improve their lives as well. They should be a part of your why!

Let's identify your WHY. And I probably should have put the why before the core, but no, your core is the foundation of who you are and your why are the things and the people that are included in your core. When thinking about your WHY you must strongly consider what or who motivates you to live a better life and it must be so strong that it pushes you even when you don't feel like moving.

So where does your WHY come from? Sometimes, your WHY can be how you were raised and having a desire to have a better life or your why could be to provide a better life for your family. Your WHY can be born out of pain that you never want to feel again. Your WHY can also come from a situation from your past that you don't want to see repeated in your future. Lastly, your WHY can be the vision you have for your future no matter how big.

So when you think of your why, you should feel awful. Yes! I said, awful. You should feel awful if you're not doing something everyday to accomplish your goal. Your why should bring tears to your eyes when you think about your dreams coming true, and they should also bring tears to your eyes when you think about letting yourself down and those who are dependent on you to make their lives better.

Now let's talk about what you are dreaming about. The size of your next paycheck, your next house, your next neighborhood, your next car, your next vacation, and the depth of your future bank account, it's all waiting on you. If you accomplish your goals and improve those areas in your life, then the people who are depending on you will also have an improved life as well.

These little kiddos are my sons and my reasons for everything. They are currently 23, 21 and 16 years old. I want to give my children opportunities that I didn't have growing up or as a young adult. I want to create generational wealth for my sons and their families when that time comes. I want to be able to help them with down payments for their homes and help them with

15

their children's college tuition, without worrying about what's left in my bank account. There is so much I want to do for them and generations to come.

On the surface, financial freedom, generational wealth, and beautiful vacations are the goals I've set for myself and my "why" will continue to motivate me to accomplish my goals.

This is my mother, and she raised me all by herself and she did such an amazing job. When I left for college, she also enrolled in college herself and we graduated one week apart. I am one proud daughter, and she is my SHERO. It is my goal to travel with her and continue to laugh with her.

This is my uncle. Ever since I was a little girl, I have followed him around and always wanted to go where he was going and do what he was doing. And when I tell you he is a boss, oh my gosh, he is a boss. And I just wanna do business with him. I want to learn all I can from him. I've always wanted to be able to do business with him and now I have that opportunity.

So that's it! So that's why I get up and go hard every day. I hope this chapter has helped you to identify your wife for everything. I hope this chapter has given you the confidence to know that where you are right now doesn't have to be where your life remains. Now keep reading and let's change your life.

My Broken Moment:

_____

_____

_____

_____

_____

Now that you feel that, let's get to work!

CHANGE

So what needs to change in your life?

I'll go first and tell you what I needed. I needed not to be broke. I no longer wanted to live paycheck to paycheck. I wanted to have a savings. I wanted to buy my children, whatever they needed when they needed it. I wanted to have enough money to buy groceries. A lot of groceries - you know my story. LOL! I wanted to take my family on vacation, and I wanted to feel independent, again. That may seem simple to you, but it was major for me, I knew that those desires would not come true unless I made some serious changes in my life. And man, did I make some changes, in spite of any resistance I experienced along the way.

Now it's your turn. Write down everything that needs to change in your life. Be honest with yourself. No matter how long the list is, just be honest. And once you make that list, the changes won't seem so hard.

What needs to change?

_____

_____

_____

_____

_____

5 Years From Now

Now that you clearly know what moment broke you down and woke you up at the same time. Now that you know what needs to change in your life, the next part should be easy. In fact, it should be fun!

Write down where you see yourself in the future. Think big and dream even bigger!

Five Years from Now:

_____

_____

_____

_____

_____

POWER WORD

The Power Word is Triumph.

Triumph—it's a word that carries the weight of victory and the essence of unyielding determination. As I reflect on my journey, triumph has been the guiding force that propelled me through every obstacle and propelled me to conquer the seemingly insurmountable.

Triumph is not just about the end result; it's about the relentless pursuit of success, even in the face of adversity. It's about embracing challenges with unwavering courage and pushing through the darkest moments, knowing that on the other side lies the sweet taste of victory.

In my pursuit of greatness, I've encountered numerous hurdles that could have easily broken my spirit. But triumph is not just about avoiding obstacles—it's about rising above them, stronger and more resilient than before. Each setback I faced became an opportunity for growth, a chance to learn, adapt, and improve.

Triumph is the culmination of every small victory, every step forward, and every refusal to back down. It's the euphoria that courses through your veins when you overcome the odds and achieve what others thought impossible. It's about proving to yourself that you are capable of greatness and worthy of success.

Through triumph, I've learned that success is not just about talent or luck—it's about perseverance and a willingness to keep going, no matter how tough the journey may seem. Triumph is the result of countless hours of hard work, dedication, and sacrifice.

In the face of doubt and naysayers, triumph has been my shield, protecting me from the negativity that seeks to dampen my spirit. It's the unwavering belief in myself and my abilities that propels me forward, even when others may doubt my potential.

Triumph is not just a one-time achievement—it's a mindset, a way of life. It's the determination to keep pushing the boundaries of what is possible and to never settle for mediocrity. It's about embracing challenges with open arms, knowing that each one is an opportunity to prove my myself and showcase my resilience.

In my pursuit of triumph, I've discovered that failure is not something to fear; it's a steppingstone to success. Each stumble is a chance to learn, grow, and become better equipped for the next challenge that lies ahead.

Triumph is not about reaching the destination; it's about savoring the journey—the highs and lows, the victories, and setbacks. It's about cherishing the process and the person I become along the way.

As I look back on my journey, I am filled with gratitude for the triumphs that have shaped me and brought me to where I am today. They have taught me the power of perseverance, the strength of resilience, and the joy of never giving up.

Today, as I face new challenges and strive for even greater heights, triumph remains my faithful companion. It is the fire within me that refuses to be extinguished, the driving force that propels me forward with unyielding determination.

Triumph is not just a word—it's a way of life. It's the essence of who I am and who I strive to become. With triumph as my ally, I am confident that I can overcome any obstacle, achieve any goal, and seize every opportunity that comes my way.

So, as I continue on this journey of triumph, I do so with my head held high, my heart filled with courage, and my spirit unwavering. I know that no matter what lies ahead, I have the power to triumph, to conquer, and to achieve greatness. And that, my friends, is a feeling like no other.

Chapter 2

It's All in Your Mind

Mind Over Matter

I know the last chapter was a little emotional, but now you are thinking clearly and feeling free. I hope by now you know what and who you are working for. I hope by now, your commitment and determination to change your life is stronger than it's ever been. That is what's going to keep you motivated long after the initial rush of adrenaline wears off.

Being keenly aware of this vital moment in your life will be what forces you to keep moving forward in your life. Being aware of who's dependent on you at all times will make you go above and beyond the call of duty in different scenarios. Remember, to change their lives means you must change yours. All changes begin in the mind first.

Understanding Your Mindset

Do you understand how important your mindset is? Out of everything that we'll be talking about in this book, your mindset is probably the most important. It's very important that you have the right mindset for where you're trying to go, for what you're trying to do and who you're trying to become.

Oftentimes, our mindset is formed long before we reach adulthood. It is shaped by how we were raised, what we were told about ourselves, how we saw situations handled by our parents and how we responded to our own situations. But if you, for some reason, found yourself struggling to overcome or keep up with life, you may have a negative mindset and that's okay. Part of the reason you are reading this book right now is because something needs to change so that you can move forward. However, if you were always in a winning position, then more than likely you have somewhat of a positive mindset.

The good thing about your mindset is, if it's already good, it can always be better. If it's negative, it's not too late to change it. Once your mindset is in the right place, the sky is the limit for what you can accomplish and how successful you can be in your life. So, get your mind right.

History of Your Workplace Thinking

Now, let's talk about the history of workplace thinking. What has been your thinking about your job? Sometimes the way we think about our job can be the exact thing that stands in our way of earning a promotion or being chosen for opportunities that others only dream about.

In this photo, you can see that I was clearly working in a cubicle with a window view of outdoors, and this role required me to clock in at 7:00 AM and clock out at 4:00 PM. I had a 30-minute lunch break and two 15 minute breaks during the day. I had to always remain on the phones, and I had a quota for the number of calls I made per day.

Basically, I was in a call center. I really didn't realize that I was in a call center until I was on the job for about two months. And I was like, Felecia, you're in a call center. What the heck are you doing? How did you get here? I told myself, you must do something different. And that's exactly what I did.

I was making roughly $40,000 a year/ $22 an hour. My check was around $700 a week. I would get "Paid on Friday and would be Broke by Tuesday". And after being laid off from a job where I made almost $115,000 a year, there was definitely some adjusting that I had to do.

Out of that $700 a week, by the time I paid one bill, put gas in the car, bought grocery for the house, and gave my kids money for the week, I was BROKE. I really had to change my mindset. I could have let this moment and this time in my life defeat me and send me into some form of depression. I could have allowed this moment to turn me into a bitter person, mad at the world. I could have allowed this moment to make me settle and accept this cubicle life as my new life. I could have, but I DIDN'T.

I took this situation and figured out how to make it work in my favor. And as you dig a little deeper into this book, you will learn exactly what I did to turn my life around and how I got promoted in a market when they said I couldn't. As you continue throughout this book, you will understand why this blueprint was created just for you, because I'm just like you. However, I'm going to help you get to the other side.

What about your friends?

Sometimes in the workplace, the workplace perspective of our friends and our coworkers become our perspective as well. So then, since they are okay with their position in the company, you then become satisfied with your position in the company. It may not seem like that's what you've been doing, but if you have a group of friends and they have negative comments and thoughts about the job, I bet you have settled as well.

Your individual mindset is so important when it comes to moving you to the next level. So, if you are allowing your friends and coworkers to control how you think about your job, stop it. Stop it, because there are several reasons why you shouldn't allow their mindset to become your way of thinking.

Stop it because:

Your goals are different.

> » Your needs are different.

> » You have different people depending on you.

> » Your potential is different.

> » You are different.

You deserve to have the life you've always wanted and the only person who can create this well-deserved life for you and your family is, YOU!

If you are unsure about the professional mindset of your coworkers, here are a few phrases that people say when they are content with their jobs and not willing to put in the work to progress their careers.

> » I'm just here to get a check.

> » I just come to work so that I can get my work done and then go home.

> » Nothing is ever going to change with this company.

> » My manager is the worst manager I've ever had, and I can't wait for the company to fire him or her. *That one cracks me up!*

> » I need to make more money, but I don't feel like looking for another job. *That one cracks me up too!*

> » I've been here so long because I just don't know what else I can do. *This one is sad to hear.*

» This company has good benefits, so I'm just going to ride it out until retirement. *Heck no!*

If your friends or coworkers are making comments like this, you need to find new friends. NO, I'm just kidding! I am the first person to tell you how important great friendships and positive groups are at work. However, if those relationships are stagnating your career progression and success, I am the first person to say run. I am not advocating for you to drop good friends, but I do recommend you tell them about this book, I'm just saying! LOL! The lesson here is to stop making those comments about your job, because that mindset will get you nowhere.

Now, if you have made comments like the ones I've mentioned, I am so glad you are reading this book. And I can't wait to receive your testimony about how your mind set has changed.

You may think it's hard to change your mindset, but it really is the simplest lesson you will ever learn.

Once I got my broken moment tattooed on my brain, everything else was easy. I no longer worried about what others thought of me. I no longer worried about standing out at work and I no longer was afraid to step outside of my comfort zone.

You may have heard this before, but outside of your comfort zone is where you find success. Outside of your comfort zone is where your belief in yourself grows, where your confidence strengthens, and where you separate yourself from the crowd. So here it is! Here are the three MAGIC steps to change your mind set at work and in life.

1. Always remember your why.

2. Remember the moment that broke you down and woke you up, at the same time.

3. Remind yourself of what would happen to those depending on you if you don't make a change and how much they would benefit if you do follow through.

I know, simple and basic, yet powerful and real! Once you start to remind yourself of these three things, as often as you blink your eyes, your life will change forever.

Alright, let me tell you about a game-changing moment in my life. After being laid off in 2017, I was determined to get back on track and started interviewing with various pharmaceutical companies. One company stood out, and I made it to the final round, yay! They loved me and my experience, and everything seemed perfect. They even scheduled to fly me out for the last interview, which was super exciting.

But here's where it gets a bit rough. The night before my flight, I set my alarm for 4:00 AM. I wanted to make sure I had enough time to get to the airport. But I allowed another person to convince me that I didn't have to leave the house so early. Against my gut feeling, I went along with it.

Fast forward to the airport—utter chaos! It seemed like everyone in the world decided to travel on the same day. I was running late, and by the time I reached the gate, the plane was gone. Can you imagine my desperation? With everyone looking, I was banging on the door, tears streaming down my face, yelling, and begging them to let me in. But it was no use. The plane was gone.

I had to call the company and tell them I missed my flight, and you can bet I felt like my whole life was falling apart. It was a real low point, and I was ready to give up. But you know what kept me going? My kids. I couldn't give up on them.

That closed door felt like the end of all my opportunities. It led to a depression, and I felt like I hit rock bottom. But here's the silver lining—I learned something crucial. My urgency wasn't the same as everyone else's. I realized that I had to trust my gut and not rely on others for my own decisions.

So from then on, if I say I need to leave three hours in advance, I stick to it, no matter what anyone says. My preparation mindset became my superpower. It's amazing how that shift in thinking changed everything for me.

After that setback, I decided to try a different sales industry, transportation & logistics. Sure, it meant a 60% pay cut, but I knew I had to keep moving forward. And guess what? It paid off big time. I may have taken a detour, but it led me to new opportunities and a whole different level of confidence.

Life is full of closed doors, my friend, but they're not the end of the road. They're just opportunities to find new paths. So, trust your instincts, seize every chance, and remember that your urgency is unique to you. You've got this! Keep pushing forward, and accomplishment will be yours for the taking.

After that challenging experience, I realized that life isn't about avoiding closed doors—it's about finding the courage to kick them open or discovering the next door that's waiting for you to knock.

And you know what? That pivotal moment taught me to be resilient and relentless. It reminded me that my journey wasn't defined by a single setback or a missed flight. Instead, it was shaped by my ability to adapt, learn, and grow from every experience, no matter how tough.

So, I took that 60% pay cut, dived into the world of transportation and logistics, and let me tell you, it was like a rollercoaster ride. But I embraced the challenge with open arms, and my determination skyrocketed. I knew I had to prove to myself that I could thrive, no matter the circumstances.

With my preparation mindset on point, I tackled each day head-on, no longer swayed by the opinions of others. I trusted myself, and that confidence radiated in everything I did. My work ethic shined, and I found myself accomplishing things I hadn't even dreamed of.

You see, sometimes life knocks us down, but that's when we discover the fire within. It's like life saying, "Hey, are you tough enough for this?" And you better believe I was. I may have had moments of doubt, but they were overshadowed by my desire to prove to myself that I was capable of greatness.

And let me tell you, my friend, greatness is not a far-fetched dream reserved for the lucky few. It's within reach for anyone who embraces the power of their mind and their unwavering determination. You don't need to wait for the perfect circumstances or the green light from others. No, you can create your own opportunities and craft your own path.

So, if you've ever felt like I did when that door closed on me, take heart. It's not the end, but a chance to redirect and find the path that's meant for you. Listen to your instincts, follow your passion, and take those leaps of faith, even if others doubt you. Your journey is unique, and it's yours to shape.

Now, you might be wondering how the story ends, right? Well, spoiler alert—I made it back into the pharmaceutical industry! Oh yes, after those years of growth in transportation, my experience and mindset caught the attention of another pharmaceutical company. They recognized my worth, and this time, there was no missed flight to stand in my way.

Life is full of ups and downs, but it's how we navigate those challenges that define our character. So, my friend, let this chapter in your life be about accomplishment, about taking control of your destiny, and about embracing every closed door as an opportunity to find your true path.

You have what it takes to accomplish anything you set your mind to. It might not always be easy, but nothing worth having ever comes without a little sweat and tears. Keep pushing forward, stay true to yourself, and remember, your mindset is the key to unlocking the door to your dreams. Now go out there and make it happen! You've got this!

POWER WORD

The Power Word is Accomplish

In the journey of accomplishment, the power of the mind reigns supreme. As I immerse myself in the depths of my thoughts and beliefs, I realize that my mindset is the cornerstone of my success. It is the guiding force that

propels me towards my goals, fuels my determination, and empowers me to rise above any challenge.

My mindset, like many others, was forged through years of experiences, upbringing, and the influence of those around me. However, I recognized that certain patterns of thinking were hindering my progress, preventing me from reaching my full potential. I had to acknowledge that I couldn't achieve greatness if I allowed negative thoughts and complacency to control my actions.

Breaking free from the shackles of a limiting mindset was not an overnight transformation. It required introspection, self-awareness, and a willingness to challenge my own beliefs. I realized that I couldn't blame my circumstances or external factors for my lack of progress—I had to take responsibility for my own life.

In one phase of my journey, I found myself feeling stuck in a job. The work environment felt suffocating, and it seemed like I was destined to remain confined to a cubicle forever. But in that moment, I had an awakening—a realization that I could change my mindset and, in turn, change my life.

I decided to shift my focus from self-doubt to self-belief. I started embracing challenges as opportunities to learn and grow, viewing setbacks as steppingstones to success. Instead of settling for mediocrity, I aspired for greatness, setting my sights on new goals and uncharted territories. No matter where I worked, I chose to surround myself with individuals who supported my ambitions and shared a growth-oriented mindset.

Understanding my "why" became my anchor—the driving force that pushed me beyond my comfort zone. I reminded myself of the broken moment that shook me to my core and woke me up to the possibilities of a better life. That memory fueled my determination and commitment to create a brighter future not just for myself but for those who depended on me.

It's true that the journey to change my mindset was not without challenges. But armed with the belief that my potential was limitless, I faced those challenges head-on, undeterred by self-doubt or fear of failure. Each day, I took intentional steps towards my goals, inching closer to accomplishment.

The transformation was profound. As I nurtured a positive and growth-oriented mindset, I witnessed a ripple effect in my life. I gained the confidence to step outside my comfort zone, seize opportunities, and stand out in my workplace. The self-belief I cultivated became the foundation of my success.

I realized that the key to accomplishment lies not only in setting ambitious goals but in fostering the right mindset to achieve them. It is the mindset that propels you forward, the mindset that enables you to persevere through the toughest challenges, and the mindset that ultimately determines your trajectory.

So, I urge you, my fellow conquerors, to take control of your mindset. Embrace a positive and growth-oriented outlook that propels you towards greatness. Remember your "why," let the memory of your broken moment tattoo your brain with determination and think of those who depend on you as a driving force to push you beyond your limits.

With this newfound mindset, you will accomplish more than you ever thought possible. The power to change your life lies within your thoughts, and once you unlock that power, there will be no limit to what you can achieve. So, dive deep into your mind, conquer the barriers within, and let accomplishment become your reality.

Chapter 3

What Others Say About You

Normally I would say, what others say or think about you doesn't matter. However, in this book there are two groups of people. In this book, the word OTHERS will represent people who really don't matter, acquaintances at work, and people you pass in the hallway. The first group of others are, and I say this in the most respectful way, are those people who really don't have an impact on your career progression. These are your work acquaintances and your average coworker you pass in the hallway. Then there are the group of OTHERS who can help you achieve your goals.

It's so easy to say I don't care what they say about me, but now you know that all OTHERS are not the same.

This Section of the book might be tough because it's going to call you out on those areas that might need to be addressed. It's better to address those areas now, than before you begin your rise to the top.

This is where, you will take a real inventory of how you are seen through the eyes of others. We are going to call this your Professional Reputation. Just like you have a personal reputation, having a professional reputation is a real thing as well. Everybody doesn't know it, but it's a real thing.

This group of others, who can change your life, have a direct impact on your daily task and have the ability to develop you personally and professionally. This group of others are Very Important.

Who are the impactful others? This list includes, but is not limited to presidents, vice presidents, managers, supervisors, mentors, immediate coworkers, work peer groups, teammates, and your professional board of directors. We will talk about your professional board of directors later on in this book. So, if you are saying to yourself, Felecia of course I have a manager and a supervisor, but I don't even know how to go about networking with the freaking President or Vice President of a company. Don't worry, because I'm going to provide e-mail templates at the end of this book that I actually sent to leaders in my company, and they really worked.

This group of impactful OTHERS refers to people in the workplace who can speak positively on your behalf, even when you're not in the room. But watch this, they also have the ability to speak negatively about you if your mindset is not in the right place. They can open doors for you that you may not be able to open yourself and they can provide a blueprint to your career progression if the relationship is strong. Most importantly, this group of others can see characteristics in you that you may not see in yourself.

Allow me to briefly tell you about one of my managers from when I worked in the call center. I guess great customer service came natural to me and my manager thought so too. This particular manager would come to my cubicle and say, Felecia, can you come to my office for a second? I would go to his office and he would say; "Hey, there's a manager's meeting next Friday and we get to bring one rep with us, would you like to go to that meeting with me?" My answer was always, "of course I would". Right? And then another time he said, Felecia, can you come to my office? And I would go. And he would say; "Hey, the application for the leadership program is coming up in the next 30 days and I think you should apply. I think that would be a perfect opportunity for you to get more visibility, fill out the application, and I will help you along the way." So, when it came to the impactful others, he fell into that category. He fell into those supportive others category because he cared about me, was looking out for me, and it showed.

If your manager tells you they think you would be good for a certain role, believe them. Fly off of someone else's belief in you until you start to believe in yourself. So, apply for the role, apply for the leadership program, and call the person your manager recommended. Just do it. This group of others are extremely important to your professional growth and the timeframe in which your career progresses. The impactful others can determine if you are in a role for less than two years with a promotion, or in a role for over five years with no mention of advancement. Your mindset will determine the direction you take.

Another example of impactful others is this group of beautiful people in the following picture. Out of all the pictures that I took at my previous job, this one is my favorite. This picture was taken on the last day with my original team before I started my new job at the company. This promotion took me from $40,000 a year to around $75,000 within 18 months. When people tell you that it can't be done, don't believe them, it can be done.

Now, back to my favorite picture! Half the people you see in this picture were my immediate coworkers and the other half were mentees of mine. Yes. As a result of my outstanding reputation at work, my professional work ethic, willingness to help others, and my beast mode ability to network. There were several people on other teams who asked if I would mentor them. And of course, I said, yes. As a lesson to you, If you are willing to help others, others will be willing to help you.

As each person spoke about what I meant to them and how much I helped them, there was not a dry eye in the room. I felt so honored that everyone had such beautiful things to say about me. In addition to knowing how this group felt about me, I also had an idea of how the rest of the department felt about me as well. Due to an activity that was anonymously performed within the call center, I had a pretty good idea of what they thought.

This activity called for each employee's name to be placed on a sheet of paper for an entire week. During the week everyone had the opportunity to write one word they thought described the person on the paper. Here is what they had to say about me

- » She's smart.
- » She's sociable.
- » She's a thinker
- » She's focused.
- » She's natural.
- » She is innovative.
- » She's prepared.
- » She's professional and disciplined.

These are all the adjectives that people used to describe me. I really want to take some time on this because this is something that I use during my interview presentation. Now, you haven't heard me talk about the interview presentation yet, but that's another separation tool that you will take away from this book. You are going to use this interview presentation on your next interviews for the rest of your life. I don't care if it's a face-to-face or a virtual interview, you are going to use this presentation and you are going to separate yourself from the competition. Got It?

OK, now back to the character bubble. LOL! This is something that you can create Yourself. And there may be some other websites where you can go and create a word bubble or word cloud or something. You can do this yourself. If you are preparing for an interview, send this question to your coworkers, your friends, your managers, or your mentors. The question is, "What is one word you would use to describe me as a professional? You will then take those words to create your own character bubble or list and use it during your interview presentation.

You will create this same bubble, same cloud for yourself, and then you will then take it and use it in your interview presentation. Okay? Here's what your message to your friends should say:

Hello_____, I am preparing for an upcoming job interview, and I was wondering if you could use one word to describe me what would that word be?

In all fairness to this book, I haven't always been this amazing on the job. I've struggled in areas that I'm not so proud of. And to be honest, I struggled badly.

There used to be a time when I was undisciplined, unreliable, and unmotivated. I mean, it was bad. When I was laid off from that six-figure job in 2017, I kind of beat myself up a little bit because I felt like I put myself on the list. Although the company laid off over 900 sales representatives across the country, I felt as though, if I had only brought more value to the team and the company, I would have not been on the list. I felt like, if only I was a part of the top 5% - 10% of sales reps for the company, I would not have been on the list.

So think about where you are right now and how you are viewed on the job, what type of value you bring to the your team. You may be good but know that there is always room for improvement. I can absolutely say that I have made a 360-degree turn around and my life is 1000 times better for it. But what does

1000 times better look like for me and what does better look like for you.

So for me, it was grocery shopping. For me it was being able to shop for grocery without having to put anything back. It was being able to drop off and pick up my kid from school on time and be there whenever they needed me to be there.

Being able to pay multiple bills at one time was a real humbling feeling. Remember, there was time when I got Paid on Friday, and was Broke by Tuesday, and could only pay one bill a week. That was crazy time! I would pay one bill, put gas in my car, and then I would give my kids lunch money for the week. And then I would have maybe $50 left in my bank account until I got paid again the following Friday.

Anyway, once I was able to earn my first promotion and then return to the pharmaceutical industry, all my bills came out from one check, and I had a budget. I don't know how many of you have delt with financial irresponsibility like I have, but it's no fun. However, after I earned my first promotion, I created a small nest egg for myself by simply saving $25 a pay period. That may not seem like a lot to you, but over time, before I knew it, I had over $1000 in my savings. After that first promotion, I was able to get my hair and my nails done every two weeks. Ladies, can you imagine that feeling?

So, there it is, after I earned my first promotion, I was committed to having a closed budget. I didn't have a closed budget when I was working that $40,000 a year job. I just could afford it! In fact, I had a pair of boots that I wore to work during the winter months, that had a hole in the bottom. On the days that I wore those shoes to work, I would be very mindful not to cross my legs, in order not to show the hole at the bottom of the shoe. My kids needed clothes and shoes and their needs trumped anything that I needed for myself. However, after I earned my first promotion, I was able to start planning for vacations; even on a small budget. Now I'm at a point where I'm planning major vacations for my family and that's important to me.

Now my question to you is, if you are happy with what the "important others" think of you, that's awesome. Keep up the good work. However, if you're not happy with what impactful others are saying about you, don't feel ashamed, it's okay. Now is the time to hit the reset button and change the way you operate at work. It's never too late to change the way you do things; the way you talk to people and the way you carry yourself. I went through everything that I went through not just for me, but for you.

Write down what you've been told by your immediate managers, during performance reviews or even in one-on-one conversations. Write down what others say about the people you hang around or the people that you spend a lot of time with at work. I can remember there were several managers who would pull me into their offices and because of the characteristics they saw in me and the leadership skills that they recognized; they would worn me of who had negative reputations in the office. They would encourage me to surround myself with like-minded people, with the same aspirations.

Be honest with yourself, no matter how long the list is, just be honest. That's the only way you're going to be able to make the necessary changes in your life.

Write down what others say about you.

_____

_____

_____

_____

_____

If this story sounds familiar, feels common, or reminds you of tough times in your life, hear me and hear me good.

Your past doesn't have to determine your future. You are one step closer to achieving your goals and changing your life. Stay focused, be intentional in everything you do, and be encouraged along the way.

Allow me to tell you a story from my time in the call center. Working in a call center was a whole new experience for me, especially coming from the world of pharmaceutical sales. You know, call centers usually have a more relaxed dress code—jeans, sneakers, etc. But not for me. I had my sights set on bigger things, and I knew I had to dress for the future I envisioned, not just my present circumstance.

So, while everyone else was sporting casual attire, I stuck to my professional suits, dresses, and slacks. I saw my attire as a way to stand out. I had my eyes on a promotion and blending in with everyone else was not going to get me there! I was determined to move up the ladder within the company and looking the part was the first step. And you know what? It worked! Dressing the part of where I wanted to be made a difference.

But I must be real with you—it wasn't all rainbows and sunshine during that time. Financially, it was tough. I wasn't earning a lot in the call center, and I had three growing boys to take care of. Those kids could eat, let me tell you! One was playing football, and they were all just constantly growing.

I had choices and sacrifices to make and the boots that I loved so much was one of those tough choices. They were my go-to footwear at the time, but they had a hole in the bottom. Yeah, it was rough. I had to wear those boots to work because that's all I had, and they matched my professional outfits. But here's the thing, I couldn't afford to buy new boots for myself. It was a time when I had to make a choice between my needs and my children's needs. And you know what? I chose them, my boys. I put their needs before my own.

Even then, choosing them wasn't easy. I had to prioritize what they needed most. I couldn't even buy all three of them new shoes at the same time. It was a matter of who needed something the most at that moment. It was a sacrifice I willingly made because my children's well-being came first. But yes, I wore those boots on several occasions. It's called doing what you have to do until you can do what you want to do.

Remember, it's about believing in yourself, dressing for the role you want and pushing forward no matter the circumstances. Even in the toughest times, when it seems like there's a hole in your path, you can rise above and keep moving towards your dreams. And you know what? One day, you'll look back and realize that every sacrifice, every effort, led you to where you wanted to be.

So, let's embrace the journey, face the challenges, and prove the naysayers wrong. You've got this, and I'm cheering you on every step of the way!

POWER WORD

The Power Word is Attain.

Alright, my friend, let's dive into how the word "attain" perfectly applies to this chapter. Picture this—it's like reaching out and grabbing hold of your dreams with both hands and refusing to let go. It's about achieving your goals, no matter what obstacles come your way.

In this chapter, we're talked about those "others" in your professional life—the ones who can either lift you up or hold you back. The ones who can make or break your career progression. You see, it's not just about saying, "I don't care what they think about me." No, no, no! It's much more than that.

You've got two groups of "others" here. The first bunch—the acquaintances, the average coworkers—they really don't impact your career. Let's leave them be. But hold on tight because here comes the second group—the ones who can genuinely help you achieve your goals, the important ones.

Attaining success in your professional life is not just about dressing for where you want to be, although that's essential too. It's about building your Professional Reputation. That's right, my friend, just like you have a personal reputation, you also have a professional one. And trust me, it's the real thing. These "others" have their eyes on you, and they can make all the difference.

Let's talk about the impact of these "important others." We're talking about presidents, vice presidents, managers, supervisors, mentors, coworkers—the ones who can open doors you might not be able to open yourself. They can help you develop both personally and professionally, and they can see qualities in you that you might not even recognize. That's the power they hold in your career.

So, how do you attain the approval of these influential folks? It starts with honesty, my friend. Take a real inventory of how you're perceived by them. Ask for feedback, even if it's not all roses and sunshine. Embrace the truth and use it to make those necessary changes.

Here's a game-changing exercise for you. Create a character bubble or word cloud with adjectives others use to describe you. Reach out to your friends, coworkers, and mentors. Their words will give you a powerful insight into how you're seen by others. And let me tell you, that character bubble is going to be your secret weapon during interviews.

Now, let's get real for a moment. We all have our struggles and moments we're not proud of. But guess what? Your past doesn't determine your future. You can attain success, no matter where you come from or what challenges you've faced.

Financial struggles? I've been there too. But I made the choice to prioritize my children's needs over my own. And through determination and a closed budget, I turned things around. I saved, planned, and made progress. It wasn't always easy, but I knew where I wanted to be, and I was willing to do what it took to get there.

Remember, those "important others" who believe in you can be your biggest allies. Soak in their confidence, even if you're still working on building your own. Apply for those roles, those leadership programs, and network with people who can elevate your career. You've got this!

So, my friend, it's time to attain that strong professional reputation. It's time to embrace your path to success and make the necessary changes to get there. Remember, your journey is unique, and you have the power to attain greatness. Keep pushing forward, keep believing in yourself, and I'll be right here cheering you on every step of the way. Let's attain the success you deserve!

Chapter 4

Workplace Reputation 360

N ow, we are going to focus on your workplace reputation. The system that I'm about to share with you is called the Workplace Reputation 360. Not only will it change your reputation at work, but it will skyrocket your career, skyrocket your career progression. So we talked about your mindset and how that's key.

This information that I'm about to share is vital to the progression of your career. I introduce to you Workplace Reputation 360. This blueprint for change in the workplace will fast track your reputation turnaround within 90 days, that's it. So there are three parts to the Workplace Reputation 360, and I'm going to give them all to you. Then we're gonna go back and break them down.

1. You want to schedule a meeting with your immediate manager to have a transparent conversation about your presence in the workplace. Make sure you take notes.

2. You want to seek out three mentors to assist you with your Workplace Reputation 360.

3. The last and most important step of the Workplace Reputation 360, and that is your work.

Let's talk about scheduling a meeting with your immediate manager where you will have a transparent conversation about your presence in the workplace. Now, let me say this, if you're being honest with yourself and you know that you haven't had the best presence at work, then your peers and the managers around you know that as well. The first thing you need to do in this meeting is admit to your manager about the areas that you've been slacking in for the past six months.

Just go ahead and put it out on the table. Next, you want to share with them your desire to grow personally and professionally. By doing this, you're actually asking your manager to hold you accountable for what you said you wanted. Next, you want to share your desire to be considered for promotion in the next 6 to 12 months. Put it out there, let them know that you're looking for promotion, but you are also saying to them that you understand there are some things you need to work on before you even attempt to make a move. And then lastly, you want to ask for recommendations on areas that need to be improved and be specific about what actions you should take to make those improvements.

For example, if your manager says to you, I would like for you to be more of a leader on the team, ask them, how do I do that? How do you recommend I go about becoming more of a leader on the team? Don't pretend to know all the answers. Your leadership style may look different than what they are needing and looking for in skills set. Let you manager know, that you really want to have an impact and fill in where there are gaps.

So, the second part of turning your reputation around, is you want to seek out three mentors to assist you with your Workplace Reputation 360. The first mentor is a peer mentor. Now this may feel a little uncomfortable at first, but if you're truly considering asking them to be a mentor of yours, then they must be doing something right. This person needs to already be performing in a way that others are taking notice.

If this person is always at the top of the list. If they're the person who is meeting all the metrics, meeting all the quotas, if they have good relationships with all the managers in the department, then YES, that is the person that you need to be connected to.

And the fact that they are a peer and not a manager or your manager's manager or a director, that's going to also make it a little less intimidating. So go for it!

The second mentor is a manager mentor. This should be a manager other than your immediate manager. This will give you a different perspective on what it means to show up as an outstanding employee.

Now don't worry. You should already have a regular scheduled meeting with your immediate manager. And as long as you let your manager know in that first meeting, what you're trying to do and how you're trying to change your reputation, they will understand you seeking out an additional upper-level mentor. Okay? Also, by asking other managers to mentor you, you're also actually building advocates for yourself. And at some point, it may seem like you have more than one manager and that part sucks. But trust me, it will all be worth it!

I get it. Listen, I had my manager and probably three other managers who were mentoring me because I really wanted to understand how they became managers. I wanted to understand their journey. I wanted to understand what I needed to do to possibly be in their position one day. It really helped to be able to have different perspectives on how I was able to do that or what I needed to do. These managers, in addition to becoming your advocates, they become, what's called your **Board of Directors**. This is a group of people who are really going to have your best interest at heart. They can bring your name up in rooms that you're not even in. They can recommend you for positions that you know, nothing about. Finally, they can recommend you move to different departments that you're not even aware of.

Now, in my opinion, the next mentor should be an Executive Mentor. This mentor is the most important. So this should be someone in leadership, at least two levels above your immediate manager. In my opinion, this person should be a president, a vice president or a director. Once again, don't panic. Remember I'm giving you these email templates. Quick story… Right after I earned my first promotion, the company hired a female President to run a very important department. I had just gotten the call that I was hired, so my confidence level was through the roof. I sent the new president an email and the subject line simply said, CONGRATULATIONS on your new role! What person doesn't want to hear Congratulations?

So anyway, once I sent that email to her, probably within 24 to 72 hours, she responded, and I was able to get on her calendar. This was at the beginning of COVID, right when they said go work from home. She was one of my first virtual meetings.

Before that meeting, I made sure to go to her social media sites, I looked up any articles that were written about her. I tried to find out what her professional philosophy was and any other information about her career progression journey. I did my research so that I could be prepared for our conversation.

If you have a relationship with a president, vice president or director, they can actually select you for a position that no one even knows about. They can create roles for you. So having an executive on your Board of Directors is super important!

So don't be afraid, push yourself. Don't be afraid to put yourself out there. Don't be afraid to reach out, introduce yourself, talk about who you are, how long you've been with the company and what your goals and aspirations are and ask for them to help you along the way.

So, the last and most important step of the Workplace Reputation 360 is *"your work"*. I know I said your executive mentor was important and they are, but this is everything that you can do.

So, we're going to go through these and I'm really gonna break them down. And I really want you to have an open mind to what I'm saying.

Okay. The **first** thing is, I want you to show up 15 minutes early to work. I had to be at work at 7:30. So I would try to get to work not at 7:27, not at 7:28, not walking through the door at 7:30, but I would get there about 7:15, because here's what has to happen. You have to put your bags down. You have to maybe go to the restroom. You may want to get a cup of coffee. If there is a cafeteria in your building, you may want to go and get breakfast or something. But I would get there at 7:10, 7:15 so that I could do all of those things, chit chat with a friend or two on my way to the restroom, but I would be back at my desk at 7:30, ready to go headphones on, smile on. Okay? But, there would be other people who would come in at 7:28, 7:29, and then they would do all those things. And then they wouldn't even really get started on their day until like eight o'clock. So if that's what you're doing, you gotta stop that because if you know that you're doing it, then your manager sees it too. And that's just not a good look in a manager's eyes if you are trying to go to the next level.

Number **two**. You want to stay five minutes late. Most managers have to stay after everyone leaves. So our day ended at 4:00 PM. Some people in my department would begin to pack up at 3:45, they were packing bags, closing computers, and putting purses on their shoulders. When four o'clock hit, they were ready to dash out the door and there were plenty of days I felt that way. But I wouldn't start until around 3:55, closing things out and packing my bag.

While everybody else began to leave at 4:00pm, I would stay behind. And right at 4:05, I would get up from my desk and I'll make sure to walk past my manager's office. And I would say, see you later, have a good night, and see you in the morning. And he would say, oh, see you tomorrow, Felecia. Listen, I guarantee you, they will look at you and at their clock and say, oh my goodness, it's 4:05. So that's a good thing because you're showing that your job is important to you. This additional time will also allow for you to strengthen the relationship with your manager.

Next, you want to exceed any metrics that are being measured in your department. So, we're talking about quotas for calls, emails, cases, meetings, reports, consultations, whatever is being measured for performance. If you have to be on the phone and the quota is 15 calls a day, do 17. If you have to send 10 emails a day, send 12. If you must write five reports a day, write six. Go the extra mile because it's being measured. Then if you're doing just a little extra, if you're doing a little bit more, then your metrics are going to outpace everyone else on your team, in your department, or in your region, whatever entity you are being compared to as a measure of success.

Next you wanna volunteer for committees that bring visibility to you and your work. So those committees could be anything where you're the representative for your team, or if you're the representative for the region, or if you are the representative for that state. Volunteer for things like that because that's going to bring visibility to you and your awesomeness. And if you do a good job, they're gonna say, oh, who is that girl or who is that guy? They really spoke up in the meeting. I like what they had to say. I really like their concept for the project. I really admire the way to listened. When you are trying to change your life, it is important to have as much visibility as possible.

Next, you want to take notes in meetings and ask questions after the meeting. If there's something that you didn't understand, ask questions. Leaders love for people to ask questions because they want to make sure that what they're sharing is being heard correctly and is understood.

Next, you don't want to hang out at the water cooler, nothing good ever happens at the water cooler. Stay away from the water cooler gossip! That's mess. Stay away from it! Don't put your name in it!

Next, do not participate in workplace drama or gossipy conversations. Those conversations get around to peers, but they also get back to managers and you don't want your name associated with any of that. Got it!

Lastly, I want you to smile. Even if you're walking down the hall, smile. You appear more approachable and you, you appear kind. People don't mind talking to you and they don't mind listening to you as well. I know this seems like a lot to do, and maybe even a little silly. I get it. I understand. However, when you think about how you will feel, when you accomplish your goal, hopefully it all seems worth it. When you think about how these steps could change the future of your family, you're going to feel amazing. And when you think about all those things, the steps that I've given you, they should seem easy to you.

I mean, you must remember why you purchased this book. You purchased this book because you need a change in your life, you don't want to be in the same position, the same spot this time next year, you just don't want that. I don't want that for you. You have to remember whose life you're changing. You're not only changing your life, but you're changing the lives of those around you. So these steps should seem easy. And I know when I was going through all of this at work and I was following these steps and I was doing these things, there were people that would say, Felecia, does it take all that? Heck yes, it does! It does take all that because I'm trying to change my life and I'm the only one who can do it.

Another one of my favorite quotes that I absolutely live by, like for real this time (LOL), I live by this one and it's by Oprah Winfrey.

QUOTE:

"Sometimes we do what we have to do until we can do what we want to do."

This is true. And it's called sacrifice. And sometimes when you are chasing a goal and you're chasing your dreams and you're trying to chase your life, you have to make some sacrifices in the beginning so that you can have the reward in the end.

So take a look at this picture. That picture was taken the morning that I was about to give a speech on a very large stage, as a part of a leadership program that I was participating in at work. I had to be at work at 7:30. If you look at my face, my makeup was flawless because I was in the makeup girls chair that morning at 6:15am.

I saved some money, and I bought a new suit, and I got my hair trimmed. I was ready for the day. I was ready! Did I have a whole lot of money to go buy a suit? Nope. Did I have a lot of money to go get my makeup done? Nope. However, that was a sacrifice that I made so that I could have the reward in the end.

Everything I shared with you in this chapter is vital. It's vital to what you need to change your life. It's vital to what you need to change your reputation at work. It's vital to take your career to the next level. It's vital! Vital means it's necessary. It has to happen. And I'm telling you everything that I did to change my life, to change the way I was perceived at work. It changed everything for me. And if you would apply the same principles, it will change everything for you.

Apply everything that I've taught you in this chapter, your life will change as well. To those around you, it will seem like it changed overnight, but only you will know how hard you worked. And if you don't have anyone in your life right now who is your support system, who is not telling you that they believe in you; let me tell you, I believe in you, you got this, you can do this, all the sacrifices that you've made, they have been for this moment right now. You can do this! I promise I've done it. And I've been where you are right now. I've done it. I'm living in it right now. I'm walking in it right now. You got this, I believe in you. Now it's time for you to believe in yourself.

What Do You Say About Yourself

In this section, we're going to talk about what you say about yourself. We've had enough of what others say about you. Now, we're going to focus on what you say about yourself. And like I said, we've spent a lot of time on what others think of you, but what really matters is what you think of yourself, what you tell yourself every morning when you wake up, what you tell yourself every morning when you get in the car to drive yourself to work, what you tell yourself when you get home, and what you tell yourself when your day is done, that's what matters. And if it's not good, then we have to change it.

Write down as many things about yourself that you love. And then write down a few things that you don't love so much.

Notice, I didn't say hate about yourself, or don't like about yourself. This moment is about loving yourself enough to recognize what needs to change and loving yourself enough to make the changes. And that's a hard thing to do when you know, you're not right in some areas. That's a hard thing to admit, but we've focused on the negative way too long and it's time to fall in love with yourself again. And that's possible!

Write down what you say about yourself.

_____

_____

_____

_____

_____

So let me tell you a little bit about the mindset that worked for me. It may sound a little harsh, sorry, but you already know I was on a mission to change my life.

While working in the call center, the first thing I knew was I had the most experience in that department. However, I was a 40 something year old woman, having to hit the restart button in life. I knew I had the most experience and I knew that if I showed that, then that would shine. My outstanding customer service, work ethic, and business acumen would stand out among the crowd. I also knew that I wasn't intimidated by executive leadership because I viewed them as human like me. Remember, I was coming from an industry where I was responsible for talking to doctors all day. Years ago, I accepted the fact that those in authority or in leadership, put their pants on one leg at a time, just like me. They brushed their teeth the same way I brushed mine. Hey, a few of them were the same age as me. So, what was

I going to be intimidated by? Don't be intimidated by leadership. They are just like you, just with a little more experience. LOL!

My mindset consisted of doing as much networking as possible, using my company volunteer hours to explore other career options within the company, and preparing at least 8 months in advance for interviews. Therefore, when I hit my eligibility mark to apply for other jobs, I would be ready. For those who be competing for the same job as me in the future, they had no idea of what I was doing behind the scenes. All my competition knew was what I told them and what I chose to show them. You don't have to tell other people what you're doing behind the scenes. Got it? All right. And then lastly, this is the harsh part, I knew I was not at work to make friends.

I was there to bring awareness to everything great about me and my work ethic. I was not there to go to happy hours. I was not there to go everywhere in the office with each other, and I wasn't trying to be on certain teams with my favorite people. I did that in middle school. I did that in high school. I did that in college, even.

I was there to change my life and it just so happened that I LOVED my immediate co-workers! One of my executive mentors gave me a piece of advice that I will take with me wherever I go, and I want to share it with you.

QUOTE:

"In Everything You Do, Always Strive to be the Sparkle in Their Eyes." — Executive Mentor

And to me, that meant putting my best foot forward to represent myself, the company, and the department.

Now, some people may say, oh, that's drinking the Kool-Aid. No, it's not. If you work for a company and you truly love what you do, you become a part of the culture. You become a part of the environment. That's just what you do. You shouldn't have that attitude of I'm just here to get a check. No, this, these are the people who saw something in you and said, come work for us. Come help us build our company. Come help us build our business. Come help us have a better relationship with our customers.

So don't look at it in a negative way, represent yourself, represent the company, represent the department. There's nothing wrong with that! Focus on yourself. Look at that list that you wrote down. I want you to glance at the things that you don't love so much, but I want you to **STUDY** the things that you love about yourself. I want you to study the things that are great about you. Okay. This is it. You got this. You can do this. It's not easy, but you got it.

I absolutely love sharing my story because it truly showcases the power of going above and beyond while moving in silence. My journey towards my first promotion began almost a year in advance, but instead of immediately diving into interview preparation, I focused on networking and building meaningful connections. While meeting with vice presidents and directors, I sought to understand their professional journeys, while also establishing rapport with them. But I didn't stop there; I utilized my volunteer hours at work to explore different departments, searching for potential growth opportunities.

Then, one day, it happened—the job posting that I had been waiting for appeared on the job board, and it was a global position that everyone seemed to want. The timing couldn't have been more perfect because I was finally eligible to apply for the job. Without hesitation, I submitted my application, fueled by the confidence I had gained from my extensive preparation.

However, there was an interesting twist to the story. I learned from a close friend that there was another candidate vying for the same position, and he seemed extremely self-assured about securing the job. He even mentioned that he wasn't worried about me, as he believed the position was already in his grasp.

As the interview phase approached, I asked my friend about the other candidate's interview schedule, and she revealed that he had suddenly withdrawn from the competition. It seemed that my reputation had preceded me, and word of my networking efforts and dedication had reached him. Perhaps he felt intimidated by the groundwork I had laid, and he decided not to face the challenge after all.

This experience taught me a powerful lesson about the significance of a strong workplace reputation. By dedicating time and effort to build genuine connections, continuously improving myself, and showcasing my commitment through hard work, I had unknowingly positioned myself for success.

Reflecting on my journey, I realized the immense power of moving silently towards my goals and letting my actions and reputation speak for themselves. The process of self-improvement, networking, and building relationships truly paid off, propelling me towards my career advancement.

I hope my story can inspire others to embrace the journey of reputation-building and self-improvement. By following the Workplace Reputation 360 blueprint and adopting a proactive approach to our careers, we can all position ourselves for success and confidently pursue our dreams. Remember, your reputation is a game-changer, and with dedication and foresight, you can achieve greatness in your career, just as I did.

POWER WORD

The Power Word is Gain.

In Chapter 4, the word "Gain" becomes a guiding principle that underpins the entire narrative of career progression and workplace reputation. The Workplace Reputation 360 system introduced in this chapter is centered around the idea of gaining advantages, recognition, and personal growth in the workplace.

The chapter emphasizes the proactive steps individuals can take to improve their reputation and elevate their career trajectory. The word "GAIN" serves as an acronym for the three essential components of the system:

> » Growth: The chapter encourages readers to focus on personal and professional growth. This involves acknowledging areas of improvement, seeking mentorship, and actively working towards becoming a better version of oneself. The narrative highlights the importance of being honest with managers about areas that need development and actively seeking

recommendations and guidance on how to improve.

» Advocacy: Building a network of advocates and mentors is crucial for career advancement. By seeking out three different types of mentors—peer, manager, and executive—individuals can gain valuable insights, support, and visibility within the organization. These advocates act as a "board of directors" who can vouch for their mentees and open doors to new opportunities.

» Initiative: The chapter stresses the significance of taking initiative in the workplace. Going above and beyond the expected duties and showing a willingness to contribute more than the minimum requirements can make a substantial difference in how an individual is perceived. By exceeding performance metrics, volunteering for high-visibility projects, and being proactive during meetings, individuals can gain recognition as standout employees.

» Nurturing Relationships: Building and maintaining positive relationships with colleagues, managers, and leadership is essential for career growth. The narrative emphasizes the importance of being approachable, collaborative, and supportive in the workplace. By avoiding workplace drama and gossip, individuals can gain a reputation as a reliable and trustworthy team player.

The chapter narrative exemplifies how the word "GAIN" aligns perfectly with the overarching goal of transforming one's workplace reputation and achieving career success. It empowers individuals to take control of their careers, strategize their actions, and actively work towards gaining the recognition, opportunities, and advancement they deserve.

In conclusion, Chapter 4 beautifully weaves the word "GAIN" into its fabric, illustrating how a proactive mindset and a focus on growth, advocacy, initiative, and relationship-building can lead to remarkable transformations in the workplace. By embracing the principles of the Workplace Reputation 360 system and applying the concept of "GAIN" in their professional lives, readers can confidently propel their careers to new heights and achieve their aspirations.

Chapter 5

Career Exploration

Welcome to Chapter 5, where we delve deep into the realm of self-discovery and charting your course towards unparalleled success. It's time to assess whether your current position aligns with your aspirations or if there's a more fitting path awaiting you. These questions are the key to unlocking the door to your dream career, so let's embark on this transformative journey together.

Now, I won't sugarcoat it—honesty is crucial here. The answers you provide are solely for your benefit, allowing you to determine if you're in the right company, industry, or if it's time to soar towards new horizons.

Let's tackle some essential questions:

- » Where do you currently work?
- » Do you like your job?
- » Do you love your job?
- » Have you applied for other positions at your company?
- » Were you chosen for the position you applied for?

Embrace the process of self-exploration. If you didn't get the opportunity to interview for an internal position, reach out to the manager or director to obtain valuable feedback. Trust me, hearing constructive criticism isn't always easy, but it's essential for your personal and professional growth. Embrace it, learn from it, and use it as fuel to propel yourself forward.

On the other hand, if you were chosen for the position, take note of the feedback about why you were the chosen one. Embrace the positive remarks while seeking ways to continuously improve and shine even brighter.

Now, let's delve into what may have stood in your way of progress:

» Has it been your own mindset?

» Has it been your workplace reputation?

» Has it been fear?

By identifying these obstacles, you empower yourself to conquer them and pave the way for your ascension.

Next, we explore your challenges within your current job:

» Are you in a position that doesn't fully utilize your skills?

» Are you yearning for a role that allows you to showcase your creativity?

» Does your job feel more written and less verbal, or vice versa?

Knowing your challenges will guide you towards a role that aligns perfectly with your talents and passions.

And let's talk about the all-important aspect of compensation:

> » Are you being paid what your skillset is truly worth?

> » Do you believe you deserve more?

If your current compensation doesn't reflect your value, it's time to determine your desired salary—the number that ignites the fire within you and fuels your drive to excel.

Now, my friend, take a moment to reflect on your answers. Let them fuel your passion for the next thrilling section of this book, where we'll master the art of acing interviews, leveraging visuals to captivate your audience, and responding to questions with poise and confidence.

As we journey together, you hold the key to unlock your true potential, and armed with the comprehensive tools from this book, you are destined to thrive. Embrace the process, face your fears head-on, and embrace the exhilarating changes that will redefine your life.

In conclusion, Chapter 6 is your ticket to self-awareness, personal growth, and seizing the opportunities that will launch you towards unparalleled success. You hold the power to transform your career into a triumph of epic proportions. The future is yours to conquer!

With this newfound self-awareness and determination, you are ready to embark on a journey that will reshape your career trajectory. As you dive into the following chapters, be prepared to uncover invaluable insights, expert strategies, and actionable steps that will propel you towards your goals.

Chapter after chapter, we will delve deeper into the art of the interview, equipping you with the prowess to impress even the most discerning hiring managers. You will learn how to harness the power of visuals during interviews, leaving a lasting impression that sets you apart from the competition.

Furthermore, we will explore the nuances of answering questions with finesse, projecting unshakable confidence, and articulating your value with ease. You will be empowered to handle any interview scenario with poise, knowing that you have mastered the techniques to stand out and secure the position you desire.

As we progress, you will discover the importance of cultivating a magnetic workplace reputation, one that precedes you and opens doors to exciting opportunities. Your newfound skills will enable you to build genuine connections with key decision-makers and mentors who can shape your career trajectory in profound ways.

In the final chapters, you will learn to navigate salary negotiations with finesse, ensuring that you are rightfully compensated for your expertise and contributions. Armed with the knowledge of your true worth, you will confidently advocate for yourself, securing the compensation you deserve.

Remember, this journey is not just about landing a job; it's about unlocking your full potential and crafting a career that aligns with your passions and aspirations. Each chapter serves as a steppingstone towards a brighter, more fulfilling future—a future where you seize opportunities, conquer challenges, and bask in the glory of your accomplishments.

The power to redefine your life lies within you, and this book is your ultimate guide. Embrace every lesson, every tip, and every piece of advice, for they are the keys that will unlock the door to your dream career.

As you embark on this transformative journey, never forget the words of the legendary Oprah Winfrey: "Sometimes we do what we have to do until we can do what we want to do." Today, you are taking the first step towards doing what you want to do, towards shaping the life you desire, and towards claiming the success you deserve.

So, my friend, let's embark on this exhilarating adventure together. Prepare to be amazed by the growth you will experience, the doors that will open, and the heights you will reach. The world is waiting to witness your brilliance, and this book is your catalyst for greatness.

Get ready to unlock your potential, transcend boundaries, and soar to new heights. The time has come to embrace your true worth and embrace the boundless possibilities that await you. The journey begins now—let's make it a resounding success!

POWER WORD

The Power Word is Fulfill.

In this empowering chapter, the word "fulfill" resonates deeply with the essence of our journey. We embark on a path of self-exploration and candid reflection, seeking to fulfill our true potential and find the perfect alignment between our skills and aspirations.

As we answer the probing questions, we fulfill our commitment to personal growth and professional advancement. We take the time to understand our current situation and evaluate if we are on the right path or if there are better opportunities awaiting us.

By being honest with ourselves, we fulfill the obligation to discover the truth about our job satisfaction and our love for what we do. It's through this self-awareness that we can chart a course towards fulfillment in our career.

When we gather feedback, both positive and constructive, we fulfill our desire to improve and evolve as professionals. We welcome criticism as an opportunity for growth, understanding that fulfilling our potential requires constant refinement. Through this exploration, we fulfill our curiosity about our strengths and challenges. We gain a clear understanding of where we excel and where we could use some nurturing, guiding us towards fulfilling roles that leverage our unique talents.

Additionally, we fulfill our quest for financial satisfaction by addressing our salary aspirations head-on. Knowing our worth and setting ambitious financial goals empowers us to seek opportunities that fulfill our financial expectations. Ultimately, the power word "fulfill" embodies the driving force behind this chapter. It urges us to embrace self-discovery, seize opportunities for growth, and take decisive action to ensure that we are on the path of fulfillment in our careers.

With each step we take, armed with newfound self-awareness, we move closer to the fulfilling future we envision for ourselves. Let's harness this power and set forth on a journey of fulfillment, where our careers and personal aspirations align harmoniously. The time for fulfillment is now, and we are ready to claim it with unwavering determination and confidence. Together, let's make fulfillment the hallmark of our career success!

Chapter 6

The Art of Networking

Let's Get Ready to Interview…

In this pivotal chapter of the book, I will reveal the ultimate secret to success—the Art of Networking. Pay close attention because what I'm about to share has transformed my life, and it will do the same for you. Trust me; this is the real deal!

Let's start with my personal journey. Not too long ago, I was making just $22/hour in a call center job. But through the power of networking, I skyrocketed my income to over $70,000 by March 2020 and an astounding $140,000 by January 2021. I want you to visualize that same level of success for yourself because it's within your grasp.

Becoming a Networking Guru is your ticket to achieving your dreams. You will learn to connect with the right people, have meaningful conversations, and glean wisdom from the best in the business. This is your opportunity to shine!

Now, let's talk strategy. Volunteering for committees and organizations is your launchpad. Take a cue from my experience—I gave a game-changing presentation on the Art of Networking during a departmental meeting. This was my breakthrough moment, and it will be yours too.

Networking is all about building relationships with individuals who have connections to others. You have two powerful approaches at your disposal: Direct Networking and Indirect Networking. Direct networking, you reach out to your desired contact directly, while indirect networking, you leverage existing connections to get introduced.

Now, let's address some common fears holding you back:

>> "I don't have time to network." Yes, you do! It's an investment in your future.

>> "I'm uncomfortable meeting new people." Embrace the discomfort; it's a steppingstone to success.

>> "I'm unsure how to start the conversation." No worries, I'll provide you with examples.

>> "I can't think of anything to say." Prepare for the conversation and have your talking points ready.

>> "Networking feels inauthentic." Don't worry about that; focus on the benefits it brings.

Overcoming these beliefs is crucial. Adjust your attitude, be mentally flexible, and invest time in networking. Your social net worth will skyrocket, leading to incredible opportunities.

Now, let's delve into the five steps that will revolutionize your networking game:

» **Be positive**. Approach every encounter as an opportunity to advance.

» **Do your research**. Know your contacts, find common ground, and create a natural connection.

» **Dress appropriately**. Your attire speaks volumes about your professionalism and ambition.

» **Position yourself**. Strategically place yourself at events and meetings to interact with key individuals.

» **Communicate with care**. Be mindful of your audience and convey your strengths confidently.

Remember, every detail matters. Make unforgettable first impressions, showcase your commitment, and protect your brand at work. Networking opens doors, even in unexpected ways, so seize every chance to create lasting connections.

In conclusion, I didn't become a Networking Guru by reading books; I achieved it through firsthand experience. Now, I'm sharing this invaluable knowledge with you because I believe in your potential to change your life. So, embrace networking, put in the effort, and watch your dreams materialize. Trust me, it's worth every sacrifice you make.

Prepare yourself for greatness, and let's make your success story a reality. Now, go out there and become a Networking Guru! I'm here cheering you on every step of the way.

Back to the Stage! Remember the picture of me on the day I was about to give that big leadership speech? Well, let me take you on a journey back to the time when I was determined to change my life, to escape the paycheck-to-paycheck struggle, and to achieve my dreams. This was networking at its finest. It all started before I even stepped foot on that stage. I practiced relentlessly, honing my skills in every spare moment. At work, I would sneak off to the restroom just to record myself over and over until I felt confident. Out of the 20 speeches scheduled that day, I was determined to be the best, and guess what? I was! This screenshot from my phone proves I was practicing in the restroom, at work!

Yes, my facial expressions might have looked ridiculous, but this was a pivotal moment in my life. I was tired of living paycheck-to-paycheck, tired of feeling humiliated by cash advances, and tired of being financially restricted. I was tired of not being able to provide for my children's needs, tired of walking around with worn-out shoes, and tired of the constant worry about bills. I felt like just another number at work, underutilized and undervalued. That's when I realized I needed to seize this opportunity on the stage to change the trajectory of my future. So, did it take all of that? Absolutely!

Now, let's dive into some practical steps to always stay network ready. First and foremost, you need to know your "why" inside and out. Keep it at the forefront of your mind, as it will fuel your determination during every networking opportunity. Your friends might think you're ingenuine, but you know this is about changing your life. Next, always have business cards on hand for those intentional networking moments. They could be the key to impressing leaders and opening doors to new opportunities. I used to grab a couple of cards even during restroom breaks – networking knows no boundaries! LOL!

Besides, keeping your resume updated is paramount. You never know when a golden opportunity might come knocking, and you don't want to be caught unprepared. A well-prepared resume could make all the difference in landing that dream job or promotion. Speaking from personal experience, an updated resume landed me not just one, but two six-figure job offers simultaneously!

But remember, I'm not just here to talk – I want you to succeed. So, in the back of this book, under the resource section, I'm sharing my updated resume with you. Take it, make it yours, and go get that promotion or job you've been eyeing!

Now, let's talk about the power of a smile. Not only does it make you appear more personable and approachable, but it also has incredible health benefits – from reducing stress to boosting your immune system. Leave your personal worries at the door when you step into the workplace. I know corporate life might not always be kind, but maintaining composure and a positive attitude will take you far.

Don't get me wrong, I understand that life can throw unexpected challenges your way, impacting your emotions. If you find it challenging to control your emotions, don't be ashamed to seek help. Most companies have Employee Assistance Programs (EAP) that offer confidential support for personal and work-related issues. Taking care of your mental health is crucial for your career growth. However, not taking care of your mental health can be devastating to your career.

Now that you know how crucial networking is, let me provide you with four easy steps to prepare for networking opportunities:

Step 1: Find a quiet spot away from distractions to focus your thoughts.

Step 2: Relax your breathing to calm those nervous butterflies.

Step 3: Plan how you'll present yourself, envisioning a successful outcome.

Step 4: Choose to have a positive perspective and find the lesson in every situation.

By following these steps, you'll exude confidence, calmness, and focus during your networking interactions, giving you a significant edge in your career progression.

In conclusion, networking is the key to unlocking the doors of success in your career. It works not only within your current company but also outside of it. So, be bold, be consistent, and embrace the power of networking to achieve your dreams. I'm here to support you on this journey, and I believe you've got what it takes to make a remarkable impact in your career. So, let's get out there and network our way to the top!

Thank you for your unwavering patience, and I'm confident that with the right networking skills and a positive attitude, you're bound to achieve greatness. Go out there, conquer your dreams, and remember to share your success stories with the world. Together, we'll make a difference!

Networking is not just a one-time event or a temporary strategy; it's a way of life, an essential skill that will continuously propel you forward in your career. So, let's equip ourselves with the tools and mindset needed to become networking superstars!

» **Embrace the Networking Mindset**: Networking is not something you do only when you need a favor or a job. It's a continuous journey of building and nurturing relationships. Embrace the mindset that networking is about genuine connections, about giving before receiving. When you approach networking with a genuine interest in others and a willingness to help, you create a powerful foundation for lasting relationships.

» **Cultivate Your Personal Brand**: As you network, remember that you are also showcasing your personal brand. Be intentional about how you present yourself, both in person and online. Craft a compelling elevator pitch that highlights your strengths, achievements, and aspirations. Maintain a strong and professional online presence and remember that your digital footprint is part of your personal brand.

» **Be Fearlessly Authentic:** Authenticity is magnetic. Don't try to be someone you're not just to impress others. Embrace your unique qualities, experiences, and perspectives. People are drawn to authenticity because it's refreshing and genuine. When you let your true self shine through, you attract the right connections – those who appreciate and value you for who you are.

» **Seek Out Mentorship:** The power of networking lies not only in making lateral connections but also in seeking guidance from those who have walked the path you aspire to tread. Look for mentors and advisors who can share their wisdom, insights, and strategies. Having a mentor can be a game-changer, providing you with invaluable guidance and support.

» **Leverage Digital Platforms:** In today's interconnected world, digital networking is just as crucial as face-to-face interactions. Utilize professional platforms like LinkedIn to expand your network and showcase your expertise. Engage in discussions, share valuable content, and connect with industry leaders and influencers. Use this platform to research companies, recruiters, and managers before interviews.

» **Give Before You Ask:** Networking is a two-way street. Always be willing to offer help and support to your connections before seeking assistance yourself. Actively look for ways to contribute to the success of others, whether it's through sharing knowledge, making introductions, or offering your skills.

» **Attend Industry Events and Conferences:** Make it a priority to attend industry-specific events and conferences. These gatherings offer valuable opportunities to meet like-minded professionals, stay updated on trends, and build relationships with key players in your field.

» **Be Consistent and Persistent**: Networking is not a one-and-done task. It requires consistency and persistence. Stay in touch with your connections regularly, even if it's just to offer a word of encouragement or share a relevant article. Be patient and nurture your relationships over time; you never know when they might lead to incredible opportunities.

» **Practice Active Listening**: A critical aspect of effective networking is active listening. When engaging in conversations, give your full attention to the other person. Listen to their needs, challenges, and aspirations. By understanding their goals, you can find ways to add value and support their journey.

» **Attend Workshops and Seminars**: Enhance your networking skills by attending workshops and seminars focused on communication, leadership, and relationship-building. Continuous learning will elevate your networking prowess and give you a competitive edge in the professional arena.

As we embrace the power of networking and master this art, remember that we are not just building a network; we are creating a community of allies who lift each other higher. Networking is a transformative force that can lead us to victory, and it's within our grasp to unleash its full potential.

So, let's walk with unwavering confidence and embody the spirit of success in every networking encounter. Let us be the driving force of positive change, not only in our lives but also in the lives of those we connect with. Armed with our authentic selves, a growth mindset, and the desire to uplift others, we can conquer any challenge and claim our spot in the hall of professional greatness.

Are you ready to seize the opportunities that await you on this networking journey? Let us march forward, united in purpose, and make our mark on the world. Remember, networking is not just a means to an end; it's a transformative process that can lead us to unstoppable success. So, let's take that first step towards triumph, hand in hand, as we embrace the art of networking!

POWER WORD

The Power Word is Victory.

In the journey of transforming your career and claiming victory in your professional life, networking is your most potent weapon. As we've explored in this chapter, networking isn't just a casual exchange of business cards or a way to make small talk. No, it's a strategic game-changer, a dynamic force that can propel you to unparalleled heights.

Picture this – you are standing on that stage, having practiced tirelessly, determined to be the best among your peers. Victory, in that moment, becomes more than just a fleeting thought; it becomes a tangible possibility. Networking played a pivotal role in that victory – the relationships you cultivated, the opportunities you seized, and the preparation that set you apart.

Victory, in the context of networking, is about unlocking doors that were once closed, turning opportunities into reality, and making your mark in the professional realm. By building a robust network, you create a web of connections that supports and uplifts you. It's like having a team of allies, all working toward your success.

You see, networking isn't just about your immediate circle; it extends far beyond that. It's about engaging with others, tapping into the wisdom of experienced mentors, and showing genuine interest in people's lives and careers. When you do that, you open doors to new knowledge, ideas, and opportunities that can lead to your ultimate triumph.

Imagine confidently walking into a room, knowing you have the support of your network, armed with updated resumes and business cards in hand. You have an aura of success about you, and that draws others in. You create an impression that speaks volumes, even before you utter a word. Victory, in this sense, comes from the preparation, the mindset, and the belief that networking can change the trajectory of your life.

Every networking encounter is a chance for victory – whether it's within your company, at industry events, or even through online platforms. It's about showcasing your skills and talents, leaving a lasting impression, and being remembered for your excellence.

So, let the power of victory guide you on your networking journey. Embrace the confidence, the boldness, and the determination that comes with it. Allow victory to fuel your passion and drive, and know that with every networking opportunity, you're one step closer to your ultimate triumph.

Remember, victory is not an isolated event; it's a series of well-crafted actions, connections, and experiences that culminate in success. Be proactive in your networking endeavors, seeking out mentors and role models who can help you achieve greatness. Surround yourself with like-minded individuals who lift you higher and inspire you to soar.

As you embrace the power of victory in networking, you'll find that it's not just about personal success; it's about uplifting others too. Share your knowledge, offer a helping hand, and be a positive force in the lives of those around you. The more you contribute to the success of others, the more you'll find success knocking at your door.

In conclusion, victory in networking is about harnessing the power of relationships, perseverance, and self-belief. It's about utilizing every opportunity to showcase your worth, while also uplifting and supporting others. So, go forth with confidence, armed with the knowledge of networking's potential, and claim your triumph in the professional arena. Remember, you are the master of your destiny, and with networking as your ally, victory is within your grasp. Let's embrace the power of networking for our collective triumph!

Chapter 7

Mastering the Interview

Mastering The Interview

Welcome to the most pivotal chapter of your career journey – the art of mastering the interview. As we venture into this crucial territory, remember that everything you have learned so far is geared toward preparing you for this moment. Your success in the interview room will determine whether you secure that coveted seat at the table with your dream company. So, let's dive in and equip you with the tools and strategies to dazzle and conquer any interview!

Preparation: The Key to Confidence

The foundation of interview success lies in thorough preparation. No matter how impressive your resume may be, it's your interview performance that will set you apart. Here's the golden rule: preparation leads to confidence. The more you practice and prepare, the more confidently you'll present yourself during the interview. So let's break down the essential steps to ensure you're fully equipped to shine:

> » **Study Important Company Facts**: Immerse yourself in all things about the company. Visit their website, explore recent news and projects, and delve

into their company culture. Research any specific products or projects relevant to your role. Become so familiar with the company that you can discuss it as if you already work there. Demonstrating in-depth knowledge will impress your interviewers and make you stand out.

» **Craft Questions and Answers**: Create a comprehensive list of interview questions and write down your responses. Focus on showcasing your strengths, achievements, and aspirations. Remember, it's okay to add a touch of confidence and positivity to your answers, but always ensure they remain authentic and genuine.

» **Identify Your Strengths and Weaknesses:** Write down five key strengths and five weaknesses (presented positively) about yourself. This is your chance to shine and highlight your unique qualities. Don't shy away from celebrating your accomplishments and what you're still working on.

» **Develop Follow-Up Questions:** As the interview concludes, interviewers often ask if you have any questions. Prepare five thoughtful follow-up questions that demonstrate your genuine interest in the company. This shows your eagerness to contribute and fit into their organization seamlessly.

» **Explain Your Reasons for Leaving**: If you are currently employed and looking to make a move, be prepared to explain your reasons for leaving your current position. Frame your response positively, focusing on seeking new challenges, growth opportunities, or aligning with the company's vision.

» **Turn Negatives into Positives**: Address any questions about dealing with negative situations or people by emphasizing the positive outcomes you achieved. Demonstrate resilience and a problem-solving attitude, highlighting how you overcame challenges.

The Power of Show and Tell

Beyond just preparing your answers, it's essential to showcase your success and accomplishments through a technique I call "Show and Tell." By capturing your moments of triumph through photos and documentation, you visually affirm your value to potential employers. Here's how to maximize Show and Tell for your interview preparation:

» **Stand Out with Confidence**: Don't be afraid to stand out among the crowd. Always put your best foot forward, smile in photos, and be confident in your presence. Confidence exudes competence, and it makes a lasting impression.

» **Capture Your Success:** Document your achievements, accomplishments, and small wins. Ask for pictures during company events or projects where you played a significant role. Be intentional about being present in group photos, ensuring you stand out confidently.

»   **Position Matters**: If you're part of a diverse group photo, consider positioning yourself in the front. This demonstrates your ease and comfort in diverse settings, aligning with companies' focus on diversity and inclusion.

Preparing for Virtual Interviews

What I'm about to share with you is the secret sauce to success. LOL! In today's world, virtual interviews are increasingly common. Embrace them with confidence, knowing that you can still have your prepared answers nearby during phone interviews. Set up your space to have your notes and answers within reach to boost your confidence during phone calls. As you progress to video interviews, position a small sticky note with prompts near your screen, allowing you to reference your answers discreetly.

The Epitome of Success: My Journey to over $140,000

As we delve deeper into the heart of interview mastery, I want to share my own transformative journey with you. From making $40,000 in July 2018 to reaching over a $140,000 in January 2021, my path to success tripled my salary and brought immense fulfillment to my life. My passion is to empower you to reach your goals and overcome any obstacles in your way. The knowledge and skills I impart to you are not just theories; they are real-world strategies that have propelled me to unparalleled heights.

Believe in Yourself: You Are Destined for Victory

Let this be a boost to your confidence and a testament to the power of determination. The passion to see you succeed is my driving force. The journey we embark on together is not about bragging; it's about lifting you higher, empowering you to unleash your potential, and becoming unstoppable in your career.

With unwavering determination, intentional preparation, and a genuine belief in your abilities, you are destined for victory. Together, we will conquer any challenge, surpass every expectation, and claim the career you deserve.

In the next section, we will dive into the most critical part of this book — a treasure trove of interview techniques that will set you apart from the crowd. What you're about to learn is what separates the ordinary from the extraordinary in the interview room. Stay with me, and we will transform your interview skills into an art form that guarantees your success.

Remember, I am here with you every step of the way, cheering you on to triumph. Let's go forth with unyielding determination, armed with the knowledge and conviction that you have absolutely made the right choice to embark on this journey. Your victory awaits, and I am thrilled to be your guide. Together, we will make your dreams come true!

Show and Tell for the Interview: Illustrating Your Excellence

Now, let's dive into the power of Show and Tell for your interview preparation. This technique goes beyond just answering questions; it visually demonstrates your excellence and impact. Remember, if you're aiming for a promotion, documenting your success becomes even more critical. Here's how you can leverage Show and Tell to showcase your accomplishments:

» **Stand Out Confidently:** Don't be afraid to stand out among your colleagues. Embrace your uniqueness and put your best foot forward. When opportunities arise for group photos or event captures, take the lead, and suggest taking pictures. Let your confidence shine through your smile and posture.

» **Capture Your Moments**: Whenever you achieve something significant at work, whether it's leading a project, completing a successful campaign, or contributing to a team's victory, take pictures or record the moment. These visual reminders of your success will be invaluable during interviews and beyond.

» **Be Strategic in Group Photos**: When posing for group photos, position yourself in a way that highlights your central role in the success or event. Placing yourself in the center of the photo draws attention and gives the impression that the moment revolved around you. This subtle yet powerful visual cue reinforces your value and impact.

» **Embrace Diversity:** If you find yourself in a diverse group, don't hesitate to stand front and center in photos. By doing so, you demonstrate your comfort and confidence in diverse settings, a quality highly valued in today's workplaces focused on diversity and inclusion.

Preparing for Virtual Interviews: Navigating with Confidence

As virtual interviews become more common, adaptability is key. During phone interviews, utilize your notes and answers to ensure you convey your best self without feeling overwhelmed. Having your responses within reach boosts your confidence and ensures you provide compelling answers.

As you progress to video interviews, create a discreet setup with a small sticky note containing prompts near your screen. This way, you can effortlessly glance at your answers when needed. Remember, preparation is your secret weapon to shine in any interview format.

The Epitome of Success: My Personal Journey

I share my journey from earning $40,000 in July 2018 to impressively over $140,000 in January 2021, not to boast but to inspire you. This transformation was the result of unwavering determination, meticulous preparation, and a genuine passion to make a difference. I firmly believe that this success was meant to be shared so that I can empower others, like you, to achieve greatness.

Believe in Your Journey: Embrace Victory

In this journey together, I want you to know that victory is within reach. It's not just about securing a job; it's about claiming the career you deserve, exceeding expectations, and realizing your true potential. Embrace the power of preparation, armed with the knowledge that you are destined for greatness.

The upcoming section is the heart of this book — an abundance of interview techniques that will set you apart from the competition. These are not just theoretical concepts; they are real-world strategies that have propelled me to unimaginable heights. As we dive in, remember that I am here with you every step of the way, cheering you on to victory.

Let's forge ahead with unyielding determination, leaving no room for doubt in our pursuit of excellence. Together, we will conquer any obstacle and claim the success that is rightfully yours. Remember, I am here to support and guide you throughout this transformative journey. Your victory awaits — let's embrace it together!

Now, let's continue with the next section, where we'll explore the game-changing techniques that will elevate your interview skills to unprecedented levels. With our combined efforts, your success is inevitable. Let's go forth and make history!

POWER WORD

The Power Word is Acquire.

In this chapter, we delve into the art of acquiring the job of your dreams through mastering the interview process. The word "acquire" resonates deeply with the essence of this chapter because it encapsulates the proactive and determined approach you need to take in securing your dream career. This is not a passive endeavor; it requires a strategic and deliberate effort to acquire what you truly desire.

Acquiring goes beyond merely "getting" a job; it signifies attaining a coveted position that aligns perfectly

with your goals and aspirations. It's about claiming your seat at the table with unwavering confidence and making an indelible impression on your interviewers.

To acquire something implies that you actively sought it out, prepared diligently, and positioned yourself as the ideal candidate. It is not about waiting for opportunities to come your way; instead, it's about creating those opportunities through meticulous preparation and a strong sense of purpose.

Preparation Leads to Confidence: The Key to Acquiring Success

At the heart of the acquisition process lies preparation. The more you prepare, practice, and study, the more confident you will appear during your interview. Confidence is the key to leaving a lasting impression on your interviewers and demonstrating that you are the perfect fit for the role.

Preparation involves writing out your answers to potential interview questions, studying essential company facts, identifying your strengths and weaknesses, and crafting follow-up questions that showcase your genuine interest in the company. This high-level preparation is like studying for an exam; it might be time-consuming, but it's undoubtedly worth the effort.

When you walk into an interview thoroughly prepared, you project an air of competence and expertise that interviewers will find irresistible. Your well-rehearsed responses will leave them wanting more, and they will envision you as an invaluable asset to their organization.

Show and Tell: Illustrating Your Excellence with Evidence

Beyond verbal answers, the power of "Show and Tell" cannot be underestimated. In this chapter, we emphasize the importance of visually demonstrating your success and accomplishments. Documenting your achievements through pictures and tangible evidence solidifies your credibility as a top-performing candidate.

When you capture moments of success, whether leading a project or contributing to a team's victory, you create a visual portfolio of your accomplishments. These pictures serve as concrete reminders of your impact and provide powerful talking points during interviews.

Strategically positioning yourself in group photos can also enhance your presence and reinforce your significance in those moments. Being front and center not only draws attention to you but also demonstrates your comfort and confidence in diverse settings, a quality highly regarded in modern workplaces.

Acquiring Success in Virtual Interviews: Adaptability is Key

As virtual interviews become increasingly common, your adaptability and preparation are crucial. During phone interviews, leverage your notes and answers to confidently deliver compelling responses. For video interviews, set up a discreet prompt near your screen to ensure a smooth delivery of well-crafted answers.

Embrace Your Journey to Victory

My personal journey from $40,000 to over $140,000 salary reflects the power of preparation and determination. My success story is not meant to boast but to inspire you to embrace your path to victory. I am here to empower you with real-world strategies that have propelled me to unimaginable heights.

The word "acquire" embodies the proactive and determined mindset you need to secure your dream career. It reflects the deliberate effort and unwavering focus required to claim what you truly deserve. Together, we will navigate the interview landscape with confidence, leaving no doubt that victory is within our grasp.

As we continue to explore game-changing techniques in the upcoming section, remember that acquisition is an active pursuit of greatness. Embrace the power of preparation and determination as we embark on this transformative journey together. Your dream career awaits – let's acquire it with unyielding passion and purpose!

Chapter 8

The S.T.A.R.L.A. Method

Welcome to the pinnacle of interview mastery — the S.T.A.R.L.A. method! What has been known for years as the S.T.A.R. method, has been adapted by me as the S.T.A.R.L.A method. Brace yourself, because this technique is a game-changer that will leave your interviewers in awe and utterly captivated. Grab your pen and paper because you're about to embark on a journey that will forever transform your interview approach.

The S.T.A.R.L.A. method is a hidden gem known to few, but its power is unparalleled. Countless clients I've worked with had never even heard of it, but once they embraced this method, they soared beyond their competition with remarkable ease. Companies often insist on the S.T.A.R. interview technique to assess candidates' behavioral responses. However, I have taken the response to another level by adding the L. and A.

Behavioral questions typically begin with phrases like "Tell me about a time when," "What do you do when," or "Give me an example of." They aim to gauge your ability to handle specific situations based on your past experiences. But fret not, these questions are easy to recognize, and I'm going to equip you with the perfect formula to conquer them!

Now let's break down the S.T.A.R.L.A. method, step by step:

S - Situation: Start by vividly describing the situation or task you were faced with. Be specific and detailed, focusing on a particular event rather than offering generalities about your past experiences. The goal is to make the interviewer understand the context and challenges you encountered.

T - Task: Highlight the objective or goal you were striving to achieve during that particular situation. Paint a clear picture of what you were working towards, demonstrating your focus and determination.

A - Action: This is the crux of the S.T.A.R.L.A. method – the part where you shine. Describe the precise actions you took to tackle the situation. Remember, the spotlight is on you, so refrain from talking about team efforts. Use the word "I" and share your unique contributions and steps taken with a high level of detail.

R - Results: Conclude by revealing the outcomes of your actions. Don't be modest – take full credit for your accomplishments. Describe the positive results and the impact of your behavior. Showcase the incredible results you achieved through your actions and decisions.

And here's the secret to setting yourself apart from the competition: Add two essential components to your answers that go above and beyond the traditional S.T.A.R. format. The L & A:

L – Learn: What did you learn from the experience? Passively show how this experience relates to the position you're interviewing for. This showcases your self-awareness, reflection, and adaptability.

A – Apply: How will you apply what you learned to the new role? Be specific in explaining how you plan to bring your newfound knowledge and skillset to their company, making you an invaluable asset to the team.

Now, I recommend that you prepare for at least seven categories of behavioral questions, which will encompass the most common situations companies may ask about:

» **Mistake:** Discuss a time when you made a mistake and how you handled it.

» **Collaboration/Teamwork:** Describe an instance when you worked effectively with a team or collaborated across departments.

» **Going Above and Beyond:** Share a story of when you exceeded expectations and added exceptional value to your team.

» **Accountability:** Narrate a situation where you took ownership of your actions and were held accountable.

» **Integrity and Diversity**: Talk about a time when you worked with integrity or in a diverse setting, showcasing your adaptability.

» **Dealing with Resistance**: Describe how you handled resistance and overcame challenges in a situation.

» **Difficult Coworker:** Share a story of how you managed to work effectively with a difficult coworker.

Your mission is to recall specific experiences from your work history that fit into each category. Write down the entire story in detail, from the situation to the results. Then, polish your answers by eliminating any fluff and focusing on your individual contributions.

To further organize your interview preparation, consider creating a chart like mine, listing each situation you've prepared for on the left side. This will keep your answers well-organized and ready to deliver with confidence during the interview.

Through the S.T.A.R.L.A. method and your compelling stories, you will captivate your interviewers and leave them eager to learn more. Your responses will stand out, and you'll set yourself apart as a truly exceptional candidate.

Remember, I've been where you are, and I want to share my real-life experiences to inspire your success. In the next video, you'll witness me answering real interview questions using the S.T.A.R.L.A. method, so you can witness firsthand how to weave engaging stories that leave a lasting impression.

Embrace this interview superpower, and like me, you too will conquer every interview with poise and finesse. Let's transform you into a true interview champion!

With the S.T.A.R.L.A. method firmly in your grasp, you're ready to take on any interview with unwavering confidence. Prepare to dazzle your interviewers as you masterfully craft compelling stories that showcase your skills, experiences, and potential.

The S.T.A.R.L.A. method will turn your ordinary stories into captivating narratives.

Now, you might be thinking, "But Felecia, I'm not in sales, and my industry is different. Can I apply the S.T.A.R.L.A. method to my profession?" Absolutely! The beauty of this technique lies in its universal applicability. No matter your field or role, the S.T.A.R.L.A. method can be tailored to showcase your unique talents and accomplishments.

So grab your pen and write down the questions you want to practice with. Remember, this is your opportunity to shine, so choose scenarios that reflect your strengths and demonstrate your ability to handle various situations. Oh yeah, a few of your answers may fit into multiple categories.

As you prepare, remember to:

» **Embrace your uniqueness**: Your experiences are what set you apart from other candidates. Emphasize what makes you special and demonstrate how your distinct qualities will make you an asset to the company.

» **Be confident, not cocky**: Showcase your achievements with pride, but strike a balance. Confidence is attractive, but arrogance can be a turnoff. Show humility and gratitude for the opportunities you've had.

» **Practice, practice, practice**: Rehearse your answers until they flow naturally. Stand in front of a mirror, or better yet, conduct mock interviews with friends or family members. The more you practice, the more comfortable you'll feel during the actual interview.

» **Stay authentic:** Be genuine in your responses and let your passion and enthusiasm shine through. Interviewers can sense when someone is being disingenuous, so stay true to yourself.

» **Highlight your adaptability**: As you share your stories, emphasize how you've learned and grown from each experience. Demonstrating your ability to adapt and evolve is highly valued by employers.

I can't stress enough how vital it is to be prepared. Your success in the interview room hinges on your ability to confidently articulate your accomplishments using the S.T.A.R.L.A. method. It's the key that unlocks the door to your dream job.

Imagine walking into the interview room, head held high, armed with compelling stories that illustrate your value. You'll be unstoppable! Employers will see not just a candidate, but a true superstar ready to make a significant impact.

So take your time, go through each category you've prepared, and master your stories until they shine like polished gems. When the big day arrives, remember that you have the power to captivate and impress. You are uniquely qualified for this position, and the S.T.A.R.L.A. method is your secret weapon.

Embrace this newfound interview superpower with the passion and determination that brought you this far. This is your moment to shine, and I am here cheering you on every step of the way.

Now go out there and show the world just how remarkable you are. You've got this! Let's conquer those interviews and make your dreams a reality. The journey to your dream job starts now!

With your unwavering determination and the powerful S.T.A.R.L.A. method at your disposal, you are ready to step into any interview room and leave a lasting impression that cannot be ignored. The time has come to showcase the remarkable talent and potential that lies within you.

As you describe the situations you've encountered, the tasks you've undertaken, and the actions you've executed, the room is filled with an air of excitement. Each word you speak, every detail you share, is a testament to your ability to handle challenges with finesse and determination.

But you don't stop there. Oh no, you take it to the next level with the above and beyond components. You share the valuable lessons you've learned from each experience, proving that you are not only talented but also introspective and adaptable. And then, the cherry on top: you describe how you plan to apply these newfound insights to excel in the new role.

The interviewer is in awe of your foresight, your ability to think beyond the present moment. They see you as a candidate who will not only meet expectations but exceed them. Your unique approach sets you apart from the rest and solidifies your position as the front-runner for the job.

As the interview concludes, you leave the room with your head held high, knowing you've given it your all. The powerful impression you've made lingers in the air, leaving the interviewer with no doubt that you are the perfect fit for their team.

Now, I won't pretend that interviews are easy, but armed with the S.T.A.R.L.A. method, you are more than capable of conquering any challenge that comes your way. Remember, every obstacle you've faced, every achievement you've celebrated, has prepared you for this moment.

Believe in yourself, for you possess the talents and skills that employers seek. You are a force to be reckoned with, and your potential is boundless. The job you've been dreaming of is within reach, and the S.T.A.R.L.A. method is your compass, guiding you straight toward success.

So practice your responses, refine your stories, and harness the power of the S.T.A.R.L.A. method to its fullest. You've worked hard to get here, and now is the time to reap the rewards of your efforts.

As your coach and advocate, I have every confidence in your abilities. I've seen firsthand the impact of the S.T.A.R.L.A. method on countless individuals, propelling them to new heights in their careers. And I know that you are no exception.

Let's make this dream job yours, and let's do it with confidence, poise, and the undeniable power of the S.T.A.R. method. Your success story starts here, and it's going to be nothing short of extraordinary. Now go and make it happen! You've got this!

POWER WORD

The Power Word is Win

The power word "Win" is the very essence of this chapter, my unstoppable go-getter! As we delve into the remarkable S.T.A.R.L.A. method, we are embarking on a journey that leads straight to victory in your interviews. "Win" epitomizes the ultimate goal of mastering the interview process and securing the job you've been yearning for.

As you confidently answer each question, you are scoring points with the interviewers, winning them over with your authentic storytelling and insightful reflections. Your approach to interviews is no longer a mere exchange of information; it becomes a strategic play to secure your spot at the top.

You are no longer hoping for success; you are actively pursuing it with a winning mindset. Your passion, determination, and dedication shine through every word, making it evident that you are the best candidate for the position.

When the interview concludes, you leave no doubt in anyone's mind that you are the one to beat. Your performance was not just another interview; it was a showcase of your ability to triumph over any challenge thrown your way.

Remember, winning is not a matter of chance; it is a result of preparation, strategy, and belief in oneself. The S.T.A.R.L.A. method has equipped you with the tools to achieve victory, and the world awaits the impact of your remarkable talents.

Chapter 9

Interview Questions

The Actual Interview Questions

Welcome to chapter 9, exactly what you've been waiting for. The questions I present are adaptable to any interview, and all you need to do is envision the diverse scenarios that perfectly align with each query.

In this chapter, you will unlock the secrets to transforming Q&A sessions into riveting narratives of success. Gone are the days of merely answering questions; now, you shall enthrall your interviewers with compelling stories that showcase your skills and accomplishments.

As you read through to my examples, you will grasp the art of crafting engaging responses that resonate with the essence of each question. These stories will paint a vivid picture of your capabilities, allowing your potential employers to envision the value you bring to their organization.

Remember, the key is in the storytelling. You are no longer confined to providing dry facts; you are creating a tapestry of your achievements, woven with passion and purpose. Each response will exude confidence and charisma, leaving the interviewers eager to know more about the remarkable candidate before them.

With a well-planned approach, you can tailor these questions to suit your unique experiences and industry. Let your creativity and adaptability shine as you showcase your diverse skills through the art of storytelling.

Prepare to mesmerize your interviewers with your authentic and impactful answers. Your stories will transcend the ordinary, elevating your interview performance to extraordinary heights.

So, first interview question, and the possible categories are resistance and competition.

Tell me about a time when you had to sale against the competition and what was the result?

The situation: I had the privilege of launching the eighth wonder medication into the diabetes space. At the time, there was already a medication on the market, and it was performing well. Insurance for the original medication was accessible to providers, and doctors were very comfortable in writing the prescriptions for the original medication. It was my responsibility to launch the new medication above 100% performance. However, due to the provider not allowing reps to bring lunch into the office, I did not have adequate access to the provider.

Task: I had one job and that was to figure out to gain more time with the provider, so that I could adequately sell the benefits of the new medication.

Action: To gain access to the provider, I had to be persistent and consistent. First, I spoke to his office manager to find out the most ideal time to detail the provider, which turn out to be early morning before he started to treat patients.

120

Next, I scheduled weekly coffee breaks in the office to discuss the efficacy and affordability of drug A. I would arrive at 7:45am and was able to grab at least 15 minutes of the provider's uninterrupted time. The information provided was valuable to him because most of his patients were elderly and could not afford expensive medications.

Result: As a result, this provider began to choose the new medication and later switch over to the new medication as his medication of choice. He began to share patient stories with me, which in turn was building his confidence to write more prescriptions for the new medication. I don't remember the percentage of market share that I took away from the original medication, but this provider became my top prescription writer for the new medication.

Learn: What I learned in this situation was that office managers and other important office staff are key to business growth.

Apply: I will apply the same effort in my new role by building strong relationships with office managers in efforts to gain quick access to the providers in my territories, which will allow me to shorten the learning curve about the practice and grow business at a faster rate.

Did it sound like interview answers you've given in the past or did it sound like how you wish you could answer the question? If this is what you have been aspiring to sound like in your interviews here is your chance to practice, practice, practice. Here is your chance to blow the interviewers and your competition out of the water. Allow me to walk you through another question. I know this is a lot, but it will be worth it!

Next question and the possible categories for this question are urgency, overcome an obstacle or mistake.

Tell me about a time you have exhibited urgency to solve a customer problem or business related matter.

I will say this before I answer the question. I hate how this story begins, but I absolutely love how it turns out. I had the opportunity to launch a medication in the gastroenterology space to one of the highest decile primary care providers. And at the end of the conversation about the medication, the provider put me out of her office, I was devastated.

Situation: I had the privilege of launching a new medication to top providers within my territory. I was very excited about this one provider, because she the perfect target with high patient volume, was an early adopter of new drugs, and had excellent managed care access.

The first time I visited her office, I found myself giving her a full detail on a standup call, in the hallway, while she was seeing patients. And then I asked her to write a prescription, which means I tried to close her for a sale during our first conversation. She asked me to leave her office and I stood in the hallway and cried my eyes out.

Task: For the next two months, I had breakfast and lunch appointments scheduled in her office to help me build a relationship with both her and her staff. I'll be honest, for the first 30 days, I didn't mention a prescription, but she could see and sense my urgency to gain her trust through my consistency and resiliency.

Results: As a result of my determined efforts, the provider, and I built a strong relationship, and I gained her trust by taking the time to learn about her practice, not only from her, but from her staff as well. I built advocates in her office who would recommend my products, even when I wasn't in the office. This provider became one of my top prescription writers for the new medication.

Learned: What I learned in this situation was that urgency is displayed through consistency. I learned the importance of listening and how to be patient focused. I

Apply: I will apply this same effort in my new role by understanding the impact of listening to bring value on every call.

I hope this second example brought more clarity to the way you should structure your interview answers. This process may seem overwhelming at first, but just take your time to build out your answers and the more you practice, the more confident you will become. I have listed 20 additional interview questions for you to go through and build your answers around. Select the ones that you feel more confident about and you feel are more appropriate to your industry, to your company, to your experience.

> » Give me an example of a goal you didn't meet and how did you handle it?

> » Tell me about a time when you had to negotiate with the customer or during a meeting.

> » Tell me about the greatest success you've had on the job. What was it like? What was it and how did you achieve the success?

» Tell me about a time when you went above and beyond for a situation and what were the results?

» Tell me about a time that you had to deal with a difficult coworker and how did you handle the situation?

» Tell me about a time when you had to collaborate with other team members or other departments, what was the collaboration and what were the results?

» What would you say your top three strengths and your top three weaknesses are?

» What would your previous manager say that your most valuable assets to your team were?

» What has been some of the best advice you have been given?

» What was it and how did you apply it to your professional life?

» Tell me about a time when a customer was using a competition, how did you win the business?

» Tell me about a time when you served in the leadership role for a project or event, what was the role and how did you manage it? What was your results?

» Tell me about a time when you made a mistake, what was it and how did you handle the situation?

» Tell me about a time when you were under a lot of pressure at work. What was your response?

» Tell me about a time when you had to use data analysis to make a recommendation at work.

» Tell me about a time when you had to persuade someone to do something.

That is gold! That is gold! I need you to recognize that that is gold! That is your golden ticket! I don't know about you, but it was always such a secret to get your hands on actual interview questions. In my opinion, the gatekeeping of knowledge was used to weed people out of the process. Well not you, not anymore. Now you have the questions right there in your hands. Promise me you will use this book as a resource?

I cannot believe this is the last chapter. I'm a little sad. I think I'm a little sad because I feel like I've given you so much and now you are about to fly. I just believe in my heart that your life is about to change. I feel like everything that you have been dreaming about, everything that you have been dreaming about for your family is about to come true.

If you've had a bad reputation at work that is about to change. If you've had bad luck getting callbacks for interviews that is about to change. Your life is about to change. Your money is about to change. Your savings is about to change. Your ability to vacation when you want is about to change. All because you were scrolling on your social media, and you saw me or you heard my voice or someone told you about me or someone bought this book for you. Whatever the case, I hope by now you trust me and believe I have shared knowledge that you can use in real-life.

Your life is about to change all because you trusted me and took a shot to buy the book. All because when I told you that I needed to change my life, you believed me. All because when I told you that I went from making $40,000 a year to over $140,000 a year within three years and tripled my salary, you believed me. Your life is about to change.

And I just want to say, thank you from the bottom of my heart. For everyone who is reading this book today, I hope your world get better and your dreams come true. No matter how you appear on the outside, I know that no one truly understands how you feel on the inside. You are the only person who knows deep down what life adjustments need to be made. I believe in you and I'm believing for you!

POWER WORD

The Power Word is Achieve.

The power word "achieve" lies at the heart of this chapter, infusing it with the essence of triumph and success. As we embark on the journey of tackling actual interview questions, the word "achieve" becomes our guiding light, empowering us to turn ordinary responses into extraordinary stories.

In this chapter, we aim to achieve greatness through the art of storytelling. We continued to transform mundane Q&A sessions into captivating narratives that leave a lasting impact on interviewers. By incorporating the power of achievement into our answers, we showcase our accomplishments and skills in a compelling manner.

Furthermore, the word "achieve" embodies a sense of determination, resilience, and urgency in our responses. We share stories of overcoming obstacles, resolving customer problems, and sailing against competition with a relentless spirit. These tales of achievement highlight our ability to thrive under pressure and to seize opportunities for growth.

As we answer questions about our successes, mistakes, teamwork, and collaboration, we do so with the aim of showcasing how we achieved outstanding results in various situations. We convey a sense of purpose, demonstrating that we are not merely providing dry facts, but crafting a tapestry of accomplishments through our storytelling prowess.

Throughout this chapter, the word "achieve" echoes in each response, emphasizing that we are not just answering questions, but reaching new heights of interview performance. We embrace the power of achievement to leave a lasting impression on our interviewers, solidifying our position as the candidate of choice.

In conclusion, the power word "achieve" is the driving force behind this chapter, propelling us to transform interviews into triumphant experiences. Through the art of storytelling, we achieve greatness and unlock the door to our dreams. With each answer, we exude confidence and charisma, setting ourselves up for a future of success and fulfillment.

Bonus

Interview Presentation

———⟨∞⟩———

Slide 1: In this opening section, I'm thrilled to share with you why I consistently deliver outstanding results. You see, I'm not just a leader; I'm a visionary. My passion for what I do drives me to excel in every endeavor, and I take immense pride in fostering a positive culture within the team. At the heart of all my decisions and actions lies a deep commitment to putting patients first, ensuring their well-being is always the top priority.

Why Felecia:

- Passionate, Integrity, Accountable, Trustworthy, and Loyal
- Able to network and collaborate at all levels
- I Believe in Setting and Communicating clear goals
- Visionary
- Create a Positive Culture in the Workplace
- My Decisions are Patient Centric
- Coachable, Self-Motivated, and a Team Player
- Strategic Thinker and Tactical Executer
- Leadership Approach: Listen, Learn, and Lead

One of my greatest strengths is my ability to connect and collaborate effortlessly at all levels. Networking comes naturally to me, and I firmly believe that strong relationships are the key to achieving remarkable outcomes. But here's what sets me apart

— I am constantly open to learning and growing. Being coachable is not just a buzzword for me; it's a vital aspect that keeps me adaptable and receptive to new ideas and approaches.

So, let's use this slide to showcase my strengths confidently and emphasize how my visionary mindset, passion, and patient-centric focus align perfectly with the goals and values of our team. Together, we can achieve greatness and make a real difference!

Slide 2: Alright, folks, let's dive into this slide and shed some light on my return to the pharma world during these challenging times of COVID. You see, I was already working from home, adapting like a pro to the new normal. It's essential for the company to know that I've got this work-from-home groove down!

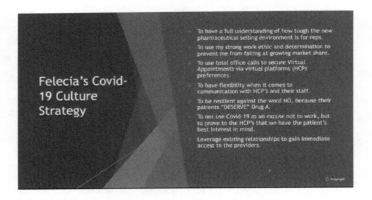

I knew the job would involve a lot of phone time, and let me tell you, my work ethic is top-notch. I'm like a self-driven engine, ready to tackle any task independently and efficiently. No micromanaging needed here!

Resilience is my middle name, and I thrive under diverse circumstances. Working in a different environment is no problem for me; in fact, I embrace it as an opportunity to showcase my adaptability and resourcefulness.

So, let's use this slide as a beacon of optimism, assuring the company that I am more than capable of handling the challenges and delivering remarkable results even in these unique times. Together, we'll make the best of the situation and achieve great success!

Slide 3: Alright, let's take a closer look at this fantastic slide that showcases my existing relationships with providers. See those stars next to their names? They're a clear sign that I've got their personal phone numbers right in my contact list — talk about being well-connected!

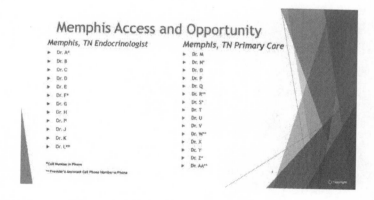

Having these established relationships is pure gold, especially if I return to the same territory. With just a call or a quick text, I can discuss important business matters, and we can pick up right where we left off. It's all about maintaining those valuable connections.

And here's the exciting part! Those two stars next to some names mean that I also have a fantastic rapport with their nurses.

In this field, building strong relationships with those closest to the providers is absolutely crucial. It's like building a supportive network all around.

This slide is truly a game-changer because it demonstrates that the learning curve for the role will be a breeze. No extensive training required here! I've already got a head start with these solid connections in place. When companies hire, they're looking to fill gaps, and having someone who can hit the ground running is a dream come true.

Of course, companies provide training, but you know what? There's an unspoken rule – they want you to start making an impact and contributing to the revenue as soon as possible. And with this slide as proof, it's clear that I'm ready to make a splash right from day one. Together, we're going to take this role to new heights of success!

Slide 4: Let's dive into my journey of returning to the pharmaceutical industry during the challenging times of COVID. The pandemic brought along a bunch of restrictions on representatives, changing how we interacted with offices. While some places allowed reps inside the building, the majority were cautious and restricted any outside contact. So, I decided to take the initiative before my interview and reached out to different offices to understand their current policies. It's all about being prepared!

Welcome Back Felecia

Office	Provider/ Nurse	Rep Access	Text	Virtual Lunch Appt
Office A	Dr. A			
Office B	Dr. B	YES	YES	YES
Office C	Dr. C			
Office D	Dr. D			
Office E	Dr. E			
Office F	Dr. F			
Office G	Dr. G			
Office H	Dr. H			
Office I	Dr. I			
Office J	Dr. J		YES	

Oh, and speaking of being prepared, you might have seen a couple of these pictures before but let me share my excitement for embracing the virtual selling environment and working from home. It's a new era, and companies looking for remote workers want to be sure they can place their trust in the right candidates.

In these times of change, I'm more than ready to adapt and thrive. The challenges of the pandemic have made me even more determined to excel in this virtual world. So, with the knowledge of different office policies and a strong passion for succeeding in a remote role, I'm confident that I've got what it takes to shine in this new landscape.

Together, we'll make the most of this opportunity and achieve great success in the virtual pharmaceutical world!

Slide 5: You know what's super exciting? A big chunk of the phone calls I'll be making in this role will be virtual! And guess what? I'm already a pro at it in my current job! They've recognized and awarded me for my exceptional work ethic. I've fully embraced the virtual world and have been having successful virtual meetings with my customers.

Virtual Selling Expert

- Virtual Selling was introduced at Company-A in December 2018
- HD Face Contest to launch initiative
- Platforms: Go To Meeting, WebEx, Teams, & Zoom
- 225 virtual meeting over a 3- month period
- 1st Place Winner of $100 Target Gift Card
- This movement set the tone for me for the rest of my time at Company-A
- Customer in the picture was the ARMY and we were shipping Riffles to Korea and grew revenue in my territory by $250,000 annually

And you know what's even better? I've got this awesome manager who absolutely adores me, and he's always snapping pictures to capture those great moments. I'm truly grateful for him and the support he provides.

With all this experience and enthusiasm under my belt, I'm ready to take on virtual phone calls with confidence and a smile. I can't wait to bring my A-game to these conversations, build strong connections, and make a real impact!

Together, we'll make this virtual journey a fantastic success, and I'm thrilled to be a part of this team! Let's do this!

Slide 6: Alright, let's take a closer look at this exciting slide where I showcased my leadership prowess and my incredible track record of launching and selling medications in various disease states. It was crucial for the company to know that I am not just confident but super comfortable with the responsibilities of this industry.

Proven Leader with Prior Launch & Sales Success

Drug	Indication	Launch	Year	Performance
Jardiance Family	Type 2 Diabetes	No	2022	114.87%
Jardiance Family	Type 2 Diabetes	No	2021	107%
Nesina, Kazano, Oseni	Type 2 Diabetes	Yes	2013	100%
Amitiza	Chronic Idiopathic Constipation	Yes	2013	127%
Contrave	Weight Loss	Yes	2015	584%
Uloric	Gout Arthritis	Yes	2009	101%
Colcrys	Anti-inflammatory for Gout	Yes	2009	100%
Dexilant	Acid Reflux	No	2015	100%
Actos	Type 2 Diabetes	No	2007	90%

This is the perfect opportunity to highlight my success and demonstrate how much at ease I am with this line of work. You see, during the interview, there might not be enough time to dive into all these details, so I'm thrilled to share it now!

I've had some fantastic achievements in leading teams and making impactful decisions. Moreover, my experience in launching and selling medications in different disease areas has been nothing short of remarkable. It's like a passion of mine – connecting with the target audience and making a real difference in their lives.

I can't wait to bring this level of confidence and comfort to the team and drive success in everything we do. Together, we're going to achieve great things and make a lasting impact on the industry!

So, here's my chance to shine and show just how perfect of a fit I am for this role. Let's seize the opportunity and make this journey one for the books!

Slide 7: Let's dive into my ability to handle any challenge that comes my way and show the interviewer that I'm ready to thrive in any environment!

You see, I've got this fantastic track record of executing tasks with precision and excellence. No matter what's put before me, I take it on with enthusiasm and a can-do attitude. It's like a thrill for me to tackle new situations head-on and make the most out of them.

Adaptability is my middle name! I embrace change and see it as an opportunity to grow and excel. Whether it's a fast-paced environment or a dynamic project, I'm all in, and I never back down from a challenge.

The best part is that I genuinely enjoy stepping out of my comfort zone because that's where the magic happens. It's like a chance to learn, innovate, and surprise myself with what I can achieve.

So, when I walk into that interview room, I'm going to radiate optimism and let them know that I'm not just capable – I'm ready to soar! Bring on any task, any environment, and together, we'll achieve extraordinary things!

Note: The pictures for this slide should be of you participating in an activity that you normally would not be a part of. These pictures should show you excelling outside of your comfort zone.

Slide 8: Now, this slide should be filled with pictures of how dedicated you are to your journey as a leader. I had the incredible opportunity to be part of a leadership program, and let me tell you, it was a game-changer. I soaked up every experience, every lesson, and it has shaped me into the confident and capable leader I am today.

One of the highlights of this journey was volunteering for the women's event. Being able to contribute to such an empowering initiative was not only fulfilling but also allowed me to network and connect with inspiring vice presidents and directors. It's moments like these that remind me why I'm so passionate about fostering a supportive and diverse community.

I'm excited to share this part of my story during the interview because it highlights not just my dedication to growth, but also my genuine interest in making a positive impact on the lives of others. Together, we can continue to create an inclusive and thriving environment that empowers everyone to reach their full potential!

Note: Make sure to have your friends or co-workers take pictures of you being great and serving in your leadership role.

Slide 9: On this slide, give examples that show and prove how others feel about you and how they have expressed their emotions toward you.

Note: Your placement in a picture is key and having a beautiful smile on your face will take you a long way and open the conversation up to talk about the moment. Show your celebrations and achievements.

Talking about these pictures during the interview will undoubtedly add a dash of enthusiasm to your storytelling. It will reflect your passion for collaboration and the incredible connections you have built with those around you.

Note to you: Moments like these remind me why I love what I do, and I'm ready to bring that same passion and positivity to this new opportunity. Together, we'll create more beautiful moments and make lasting memories as we reach new heights of success!

Slide 10: Oh, let me tell you about this truly bittersweet day captured in this special picture. It's one of my absolute favorites! You see, this was the day I was leaving one department to embark on a new journey in another. It was a mix of emotions, but this picture represents something truly beautiful.

If you take a closer look, you'll notice something heartwarming. Half of the people in the picture are my immediate coworkers, and the other half are my mentees. It's like a snapshot of the amazing relationships I've built — a true testament to my diverse spirit and natural ability to connect with everyone.

During the interview, I always share this picture and talk about the meaningful connections I've fostered throughout my career. It's not just about talking myself up; it's about showcasing the authentic relationships I have with colleagues and mentees alike.

Slide 11: Now, let's talk about the closing slide, which is an absolute gem. It's all about what others say about me. We had this fantastic activity where everyone wrote a descriptive word on a sheet of paper and put it on the wall. It was incredible to see the character bubbles forming, showing the impact I've had on those around me.

You know, an interview is a chance to share your greatness, but it's also an opportunity to let others speak for you. It's humbling and empowering to know that the words on that wall represent the trust and respect my colleagues have in me.

So, as we conclude the interview, I'll leave them with this powerful image in mind – a reflection of the genuine connections and positive influence I bring to every team I'm a part of. Together, we'll create an even brighter future filled with meaningful relationships and remarkable achievements!

This is what I would say at the end of the interview: And that, my friends, brings us to my all-time favorite quote by the incredible Les Brown! It's a reminder to always aim high, dream big, and never be afraid to go after our wildest ambitions.

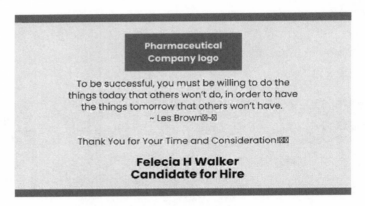

I want to take this moment to express my heartfelt gratitude to each and every one of you for your time and consideration. It has been an absolute pleasure sharing my journey, my passion, and my dedication with you today.

I truly believe that together, we can reach new heights of success and make a lasting impact in everything we do. So, let's shoot for the moon and beyond!

The Unstoppable Success Action Plan

Hey, let me share a quick story with you about my mindset during this transformative phase of my life. It's pretty cool, I promise!

So, as all these changes were unfolding, I found myself experiencing a shift in my mindset. It was like a lightbulb moment, you know? I realized that I had the power to take control of my life and make things happen. It was empowering, to say the least!

You know, a big part of changing my life was changing the way I handled my finances. I used to get paid on Friday and be broke by Tuesday because I lacked discipline and had no savings to fall back on. But once I decided to transform my work life, I knew I had to be different with my money too. So, I started saving, and let me tell you, it wasn't some huge amount at once. It was just $25 from each pay period, automatically sent to my savings account by my company.

I remember chuckling at the thought of just $25, but it was a start. One month in, I had a hundred bucks saved up. Two months, it grew to $200, and three months, I had $300 tucked away. I kept at it, and whenever I got a bonus or some extra cash, I'd add it to the savings account. Before I knew it, I had a thousand dollars in the bank, and eventually, even more - $1,500. Sure, I had to dip into it for emergencies, but that didn't stop me. I'd start right over and keep putting $25 into the account.

Yeah, I'll admit it - I was stuck in that check cashing cycle, borrowing, and paying back only to borrow again. It wasn't where I wanted to be. But starting that savings account changed everything. Suddenly, I had my own nest egg, and when emergencies popped up, I didn't have to rely on institutions or other people. I could help myself out of tough situations.

You know, needing to ask others for money takes a hit on your confidence. You might feel like they're holding it over your head, even if they're not. It makes you feel like you have no control over your life. But creating that savings account gave me back the power. I'm no financial expert, but I found what worked for me - having my own safety net, my own savings account to borrow from when needed. It was a small step, but it made a big difference in gaining control of my finances while changing my life.

You've just experienced an amazing journey through each chapter of your life story, and now it's time to take action! Here are some empowering steps you can embrace:

Chapter 1: The Power of Believing in Yourself
Action Steps:

» Embrace Self-Reflection: Take a moment to reflect on your strengths, achievements, and past successes. Acknowledge the value you bring to the table and the unique skills you possess. This self-awareness forms the foundation of believing in yourself.

» Challenge Limiting Beliefs: Identify any self-doubt or limiting beliefs that may hold you back. Replace them with positive affirmations and empowering thoughts. Remind yourself that you are capable of overcoming challenges and achieving greatness.

» Set Bold Goals: Dream big and set ambitious goals for yourself. Break these goals down into smaller, achievable steps, and create a roadmap to success. When you set audacious targets, you ignite the fire within to prove to yourself that you can achieve the extraordinary.

Chapter 2: Crafting Your Personal Brand

Action Steps:

» Define Your Core Values: Consider the values that are most important to you both personally and professionally. Use these values as a compass to guide your actions, decisions, and interactions with others. Living in alignment with your values enhances your authenticity.

» Curate Your Online Presence: Review your social media profiles and other online content. Ensure they reflect the personal brand you want to portray.

Showcase your skills, passions, and achievements in a
positive light that aligns with your career goals.

» Network with Purpose: Engage in networking
opportunities with a purpose. Seek out events,
conferences, or online platforms where you can
connect with like-minded individuals or industry
professionals. Building genuine relationships can
open doors to new opportunities.

Chapter 3: Mastering Your Mindset

Action Steps:

» Practice Gratitude Daily: Take a moment each day to
express gratitude for the positive aspects of your life.
Cultivating a gratitude mindset helps shift your focus
from what you lack to the abundance around you,
fostering a positive outlook.

» Embrace Challenges as Growth Opportunities:
Instead of shying away from challenges, view them as
opportunities for growth and learning. Embrace the
mindset that with effort and perseverance, you can
overcome any obstacle that comes your way.

» Surround Yourself with Positivity: Surround yourself
with supportive and positive influences. Seek out
mentors, friends, or colleagues who uplift and
encourage you. Their positivity will reinforce your
belief in yourself and inspire you to achieve more.

Chapter 4: Building a Winning Resume

Action Steps:

» Highlight Your Achievements: Let's dive into building a resume that shines brighter than a shooting star! Go through your work experiences and pick out those moments when you truly excelled. These achievements will make your resume stand out like a superstar in a crowd.

» Tailor Your Resume: Time to customize your resume like a tailor crafting a designer suit! Research the company and the job you're applying for, then tailor your resume to match their needs. Show them that you're the perfect fit for the role and watch their eyes light up with excitement.

» Get Feedback: Don't go at it alone; it's time to gather your cheerleaders! Share your resume with friends, family, or career advisors, and ask for their feedback. With their support, you'll polish your resume until it gleams like a diamond, ready to dazzle any employer.

Chapter 5: The Art of Writing Cover Letters

Action Steps:

» Personalize Your Introduction: Hey there, rockstar! Let's craft a cover letter that grabs attention from the get-go! Address it to the hiring manager by name and show them you've done your homework. Mention something specific about the company that wows them from the first line.

» Showcase Your Fit: Time to strut your stuff and show how perfectly you match the company's groove! Expand on your skills and experiences in the cover letter, connecting the dots between what they need and what you bring to the table. They'll be dancing to the beat of your qualifications.

» End with Enthusiasm: Finish strong, my interview champion! Conclude your cover letter with a burst of excitement and energy. Let them know you're pumped about the opportunity and can't wait to make a difference. Leave them eagerly awaiting your next move!

Chapter 6: Nailing the Job Application Process

Action Steps:

» Stay Organized: Let's get your application game on point! Create a cool organizational system to keep track of all your applications. Note down the dates, requirements, and follow-up actions. With everything organized, you'll glide through the process like a pro.

» Follow Up Thoughtfully: Time to show off your impeccable follow-up skills! If you don't hear back after an application, send a warm and friendly follow-up email. You'll stand out like a shooting star in the night sky, and they'll see your genuine interest and dedication.

» Prepare for Interviews: It's showtime, interview superstar! Research the company inside out, practice your answers, and shine like a star during the interview. You're ready to rock their world and show them why you're the one they've been waiting for.

Chapter 7: Mastering the Art of Networking

Action Steps:

» Leverage LinkedIn: Time to work your magic on LinkedIn! Optimize your profile to showcase your skills and experience. Connect with professionals in your industry and companies you admire. Engage in discussions and let your personality shine like a superstar.

» Attend Networking Events: Showtime, social butterfly! Seek out networking events, whether in person or virtual, that align with your interests and industry. Work the room like a pro, making genuine connections with a smile that dazzles.

» Follow Up and Stay Connected: Don't let the magic fade; keep those connections glowing! After networking events, follow up with a thoughtful thank-you message. Stay in touch, share valuable content, and let your networking constellation grow brighter with time.

Chapter 8: The S.T.A.R.L.A. Method

Action Steps:

» Craft Your Compelling Stories: Ready to shine like a superstar storyteller? Dig into your experiences and pick out those golden moments that fit the S.T.A.R.L.A. method categories. Write down each story with passion and detail, making sure you're the star of the show.

» Customize Your Answers: Now it's time to tailor your stories like a bespoke suit! Align each story with the interview question and the company's values. Show them how you'll bring your unique talents to their stage, leaving them cheering for an encore.

» Practice, Practice, Practice: Lights, camera, action! Rehearse your stories until they roll off your tongue effortlessly. Conduct mock interviews with friends or family to fine-tune your performance. With practice, you'll deliver your stories like a seasoned celebrity on the red carpet.

Chapter 9: The Actual Interview Questions

Action Steps:

» Embrace Your Unique Experiences: Time to let your star power shine, interview sensation! Choose the interview questions that let your strengths sparkle. Embrace your unique experiences and show them how you stand out from the crowd.

» Exude Confidence and Humility: Own that interview room with grace and poise! Showcase your achievements with pride but stay grounded with humility. A confident yet humble attitude will make you the interviewer's favorite rising star.

» Be Authentic and Passionate: Let your inner superstar shine through every answer! Be genuine, passionate, and let your personality dazzle. They'll be mesmerized by your authenticity and remember you as the interview performance of a lifetime.

You're a natural-born star, and these action steps will turn you into a dazzling interview sensation. Embrace the process with enthusiasm and remember that the sky's the limit for your career success. Let's light up the interview stage and make your dreams come true! Break a leg out there, superstar!

Thank You for Finishing the Book

I can't believe we are here already. I can't believe that you have completed the entire book. I can't wait to hear you say it worked! Felecia, everything you said happened. I handled the situations just like you said, and it worked.

Thank you from the bottom of my heart for trusting me with your future and for believing this book could make a difference. Thank you for stepping outside of your comfort zone to allow me to be your career coach. Thank you for all of the questions and comments about the book throughout the book. I'm so happy that you made it to the end and now you are ready to fly.

Now there is no turning back for you, so don't even try it. There are four things that I would love for you to do.

1. Make sure that you are following me on all social media platforms because helping others is my passion and I won't stop motivating and inspiring others.

2. Please don't hesitate to refer a friend or two to the book so that they can match your greatness! You are about to soar and if they are truly your friends, you should take them with you.

Again, THANK YOU for trusting me. It has been an honor and a pleasure serving you, sharing this information with you and being your real-world career coach!

Until next time,

Stay Focused, Be Intentional in Everything You Do, and Be Encouraged Along the Way!

I Love and Appreciate You All,

Felecia Higgs Walker

Made in the USA
Columbia, SC
10 October 2023

24216461R00095